On Purpose

by Jim Tanner

Jim Tanner

First published by Empowered

Media 2020 Copyright © 2020

by

Jim Tanner

First edition

ISBN: 978-1-7352120-0-5

To Eric Worre, for elevating the profession of direct sales.

Jim Tanner

4

Table of Contents

Jim Tanner

Foreword
By Todd Falcone

If you're wondering whether you've got what it takes to succeed in the direct selling profession, then this book will give you answers to help you change your life for the better.

I highly doubt that it's an accident you're reading this book. There's a reason, a purpose as to why you chose to put this into your hands.

You want answers, and you're curious to know what it takes to succeed in this profession.

And...let me tell you, that inquisitive, curious quality that you have is exactly what will lead you to the answers you're looking for in your business. You'll find many of those answers right here.

I've spent the past 30 years in direct sales...both in the field as a distributor, as well as speaking and teaching it all over the world.

Without question, the most fulfilling thing about teaching this business is hearing from people that say to you, *"You've made a major impact on my life and my business."*

The author of this book is one of those people. Jim Tanner began plugging into my training many years ago and took action on what he learned. And…it's because of those actions that you get to read his success story today.

I've been very fortunate to be connected with Jim throughout most of his journey in the direct selling profession. I remember the very first time we spoke, as well as the time he called to let me know he surpassed a million dollars in earnings.

Now…you get to go on that journey with him, as he shares with you his personal life story of going from delivering furniture and barely making ends meet, to having the freedom to live life however he sees fit.

If you're wondering whether this business is for you, or whether you've got what it takes to make it…Jim will provide you with direct answers to the most common thoughts or challenges people have in this business.

He literally takes you through a process of answering what are undoubtedly the biggest things that hold people back from success. There are so many misconceptions people have about creating success in direct sales. And, Jim bluntly covers them and provides you with answers based on his personal experience. There's nothing more empowering than learning from real-life experience...and Jim does that for you.

This book will change your thinking and as a result...your actions.

If you're ready to live a life of purpose, then follow Jim Tanner on this journey of becoming an Empowered Entrepreneur.

Jim Tanner

Acknowledgments

To my daughter Olive, you were still in mommy's belly when I wrote the first words of this book. The book that those words turned into became available shortly after you turned five years old. During the weeks, months, and years in between I have imagined that someday you would read this book and learn a little more about your dad. I would have loved to have a book like this written by my parents, grandparents, and great grandparents so I could relive and preserve their history. Because we do not have those books I challenge you to live a wildly purpose-filled life and document your journey in whatever ways mean the most to you. You will likely feel from time to time that you do not have anything worth writing down, I hope you will remember that your voice is worth sharing and share it as often as you can.

To Nicola, most people will never see the poorly written and clumsily constructed version of these stories that you somehow helped me turn into a real book. Even more important, you helped me be far more honest and vulnerable with my personal stories than I dared to be on my own.

The book I thought I was going to write was more of a training manual full of "how-to" instructions. Instead, you pulled out of me a book that profiles who I was, who I became, and how I want to be remembered. You are one of the influential women in my life and I am a far better person for our work together.

To my friends and business partners Adam and Alicia Thompson, your contribution to this book and my life is immeasurable. I've had the honor of spending time with you both at our home, at your home, and on some of the most fabulous beaches around the world. When I am around you I am inspired to raise the bar on how I can be of service to others. Your example of living a purposeful, intentional, and kind life has been transformative for me. I am a better man for knowing you both.

To Todd Falcone, every day you change someone's business and life with your training and inspiration. When I started to reach out to you, you could have treated me like a customer but instead, you treated me like a friend. You were genuinely happy for me and the success I was having. It is entirely possible that today I would still be delivering furniture and living paycheck to paycheck if not for discovering your resources. I hope I have been able to convey to you how eternally grateful I am for all of your contributions to the profession of direct sales.

To Bill Charron, I have no idea why you agreed to meet with me in Poultney, Vermont to look at a new business opportunity. After several painful years which finally ended with the spectacular failure of our last business I did not expect you to want to be in business with me ever again. Not only did you sit down with me that day, you believed in my vision enough to sign up and run hard with me down a new path. I'm grateful that you were with me for some of the hardest fought victories and the most devastating losses. I do not know how I would have gotten this far without you.

To Les Brown, thank you for speaking to my soul.

To Mark Riches, the first real millionaire I ever met. My whole life I was told that the path to financial freedom depended on who you knew, where you went to school, your parents, or where you were born. When I heard your story of building your business with hard work and determination, I was hopeful that I could do it too. When I met you in person, I realized I had found the coach and mentor that would push me to reach my goals. Long before I had made the commitment to succeed for myself, I wanted to succeed for you. I wanted then, and continue to want now, to make you proud. At a training event in Cookeville, Tennessee you once introduced me as a future millionaire to those in attendance. You were not predicting the future, you were speaking into me your belief in what I could accomplish. Your belief has defined my business and my life.

To my uncles Fran, Edward, Paul, and Dale. It is my hope that you read this book and understand how influential you have been in my life. While you were working hard at your jobs, being great husbands, and awesome dads I was paying attention. You take care of your family and friends. You respect where you came from and want to leave the world better than you found it. When I would drift away from the family in search of my path in life it would be you and all of our family that would bring me back to

Proctor for a holiday or a summer evening fire on the hill. Your sons and daughters are some of the most fortunate for the dads they have and I aspire daily to be a dad just like each of you.

To my wife Danielle, somehow you make everything I want to do seem possible while at the same time subtly elevating my vision to something even bigger. From reading every draft to taking the cover photo, this book would not exist without your equal commitment to getting it done. Additionally, there would not be much to write about without your partnership in our business and your effort to craft what has become a dream life for our family. You make huge contributions to the world so quietly that people often do not notice it was you who made them. I notice. To me, you are a larger than life superhero and nothing makes me happier than watching people appreciate your gifts. I am your biggest fan.

Jim Tanner

Introduction

On Purpose means to live life intentionally. Too often we live as if life is something that happens to us. We behave as though our circumstances of the moment are not affected by the choices we make or fail to make. We have the ability to be intentional in all of our choices large and small.

On Purpose also means to know what your purpose in life is and make decisions informed by those values. Leaders in our profession describe that as knowing your *why*. To truly be successful in life, we must live in line with our authentic self and be intentional in following our why. When you understand your purpose in life, you gain clarity and power that you may otherwise think is not within your control.

Throughout this book, I have chosen the term direct sales to describe the profession that allowed me to design my dream life. While other people refer to our profession as network marketing, multi-level marketing (MLM), referral marketing or other terms I have always preferred direct sales. The definition of direct sales according to the Direct Selling Association website dsa.org states the following:

Direct selling is a retail channel used by top global brands and smaller, entrepreneurial companies to market products and services to consumers. Companies market all types of goods and services, including jewelry, cookware, nutritionals, cosmetics, housewares, energy and insurance, and much more. The direct selling channel differs from broader retail in an important way. It is not only about getting great products and services into consumers' hands. It is also an avenue where entrepreneurial-minded Americans can work independently to build a business with low start-up and overhead costs.

Direct sales has not just allowed me to make more money, it has become the vehicle to become a better version of myself. I have become an empowered entrepreneur, member of my community, husband, father, and friend. You will learn that my journey to empowerment has not been easy. Although growth is hard, I can say confidently that the results are worth the effort.

I have organized the lessons in the following pages around cognitive distortions that prevent people from starting a direct sales business or succeeding in the business that they have already started. Cognitive distortions are simply ways that our mind convinces us of something that is not actually true. These inaccurate thoughts are usually used to reinforce negative thinking or emotions, appearing to be rational and accurate, but only serve to keep us feeling bad about ourselves. I have personally dealt with several of these distortions. I have worked with hundreds of people personally to overcome these thoughts and unlock their greatest potential.

In the natural world, change occurs inevitably. When the time is right, a caterpillar stops eating, hangs upside down from a twig or leaf, and spins itself a silky cocoon. Within its protective casing, the caterpillar radically transforms its body, eventually emerging as a butterfly. The caterpillar cannot decide to remain in the cocoon for its entire life. It must pursue its purpose of flying free in the sky as a butterfly.

You are not a caterpillar predetermined to become a butterfly. You have the ability to develop and plan your own metamorphosis. Deep within are quiet whispers, or possibly loud screams, urging you to change. Unlike the caterpillar, you have the ability to ignore those messages. It is your right to bottle up or block out your frustration, impatience, and disappointment. You were born with the capacity to act independently and make choices, including the choice to do nothing.

This may lead even the most unsatisfied or distraught people to continue on with their lives without making much change. The very agency that gives us the power to transform also gives us the option to accept the status quo. I find this to be the most fascinating part of being human.

In the pages that follow you will learn about my journey of becoming an empowered entrepreneur through the profession of direct sales. You will learn how I gained control over my finances and my schedule by controlling my thoughts and perspective. I am excited to share my journey with you, but more importantly, I hope it inspires you to start or continue your own journey as an empowered entrepreneur in the profession of direct sales.

Each chapter will address a cognitive distortion I hear in the field of direct sales. Even though there are numerous examples, this book will target those I most commonly encounter. I will use each chapter to combat the distortion, sharing my own experiences along the way. Transforming your thinking is a fundamental component to success in this field, or in any pursuit for that matter. My hope is to help you to understand the importance of intentionality in both thought and action by providing you with concrete steps you can take immediately.

In each chapter, after I highlight the distortions in thinking that may be holding you and your team back, I will provide concrete exercises for you to complete. I refer to these exercises as empowered actions. I recommend that you engage with the activities directed in each of the eleven chapters where they are found. Get yourself a journal or notebook to accompany your reading of this book. You could also create a document and complete each exercise electronically on your computer or phone. Use this journal or document to complete the prompts in each chapter. Do not skip this part. Do not just answer the prompts, write them down. Your active engagement in combating distortions is key to your success.

At the conclusion of each chapter, you will find examples of empowered thoughts as well as a prompt that encourages you to develop your own personal strength-based affirmation to combat distorted thinking. Take the time after reading each chapter to write out your affirmation. You can also record your affirmations in your journal or electronic device. The important thing is that you intentionally develop these affirmations. This is an important action step that will help you combat distorted thinking and transform and empower your business. You might also consider writing your affirmations on a notecard or piece of paper and posting them where you will be able to see them each day.

The process of recording the events of my life and the lessons I have learned has been emotional for me. I am proud of my accomplishments so far and I am excited to share with you the story of my pursuit of a future radically different from my past.

Jim Tanner

Distortion 1: I Already Have a Job

"All great changes are preceded by chaos." —
Deepak Chopra

She was frozen. The man screamed again for her
to hang up the phone but she could not
move. "Nancy!" I yelled at her. She looked up at
me with tears in her eyes as I took the phone out
of her hand and hung it up. Immediately, the
customer she had been talking to called back, but
I did not answer it. Instead, the ringing phone
added to the chaos of the scene unfolding
around me. Directly behind me, there was a
heavy metal door that opened to an alley in the
back. I wondered if I could make a run for it but
I was snapped back to the reality of the moment
as the man dressed all in black pressed his sawed-
off shotgun into my chest.

My job was delivering furniture and appliances,
and I had recently transferred to this location in
Providence, Rhode Island from an inner-city
location in Schenectady, New York. I was
unprepared for the reality of my new
surroundings. I did not think any place could be
as dangerous as Schenectady, where I worked
with the constant awareness that a violent
encounter could happen at any moment. One
neighborhood, where I frequently made

deliveries, a group of boys ordered a pizza just to lure the driver to their apartment complex where they robbed and killed him. My guard was always up in that city, but how dangerous could a tiny city in New England be? My eyes were opened on a fateful winter night.

The armed men who committed the robbery wore military-style gas masks and sweatshirts with the hoods pulled up over their heads. When they entered the store, they locked the doors behind them and turned off the lights. By the time I realized what was happening, one of the gunmen had stepped into our office and demanded that I hang up the phone and go with him. I held my hands up and I was careful to avoid making eye contact. I did not want him to think I was trying to identify him. He was there for the money, not for me. As Nancy and I were pushed out of the office I held two thoughts in my mind. I wondered how many gunmen were in the store, but my bigger concern was that someone would try to be a hero and get us all killed.

I was directed into the employee bathroom where the other gunman had gathered my fellow employees and a few customers who were unlucky enough to be in the store at the time. As they forced each of us into that small, dark bathroom, one of the assailants stood in the open doorway. The ambient glow from signs behind him cast just enough light to allow us to understand our bleak situation. He raised the barrel of the gun to his waist level. It felt like there was nothing any of us could do to save our own lives at that moment. We were cornered and we were about to know our fate.

Every one of my muscles was tense, my eyes slammed shut. I was certain that this man was going to pull the trigger and shoot us all. My thoughts turned to what would happen after that. I imagined my mother getting a phone call telling her that her son was shot and lying in a hospital bed. The memory of worrying about my mother is crystal clear, but more than anything, I recall the physical tension in my body in anticipation of being shot at close range.

All of those thoughts were silenced by that terrible noise followed by total darkness. . .

BAM!

Fortunately, the noise was not the sound of a shotgun blast, it was the gunman slamming the bathroom door. The darkness that followed was more than a small, unlit bathroom. It was a black hole in which several people had just shared a near-death experience. He did not shoot. I did not die.

We heard them shouting instructions to one another as they gathered the money and fled the store. In the silence that followed, it was clear that they were gone, so we left the bathroom and called the police. They arrived within minutes, but the time felt much longer.

After speaking with the police we secured the store and headed home. Other than our late departure after the robbery, the routine was basically the same, but I was different. I went home to get some sleep, but sleep did not come that night or in the nights that followed.

The next morning I arrived for my shift, and of the employees who had been there during the robbery, I was the only one who showed up for work, which surprised me. It had not occurred to me to stay home. Some of my coworkers returned after a few days or a few weeks, some never came back, but I could not stay home. It was two days before Christmas and the store had to be open. I did not want to be there, and every night I was anxious about working in the store after dark or walking to my car after closing. I struggled emotionally but I did not leave my job. Quitting was not an option in my financial situation. I was taught to be grateful for the work. A good employee does not complain, not about this situation, not about anything.

After my dramatic wake-up call in Providence, I began searching for a better way to make a living. I started like most people would, by looking for a new job.

Not long before the incident, I had learned about the fascinating concept of passive income from a book that was popular at the time. Until I read the book, I assumed all money came in the form of earned income. In my experience, you worked for an hourly wage, trading time for money. If you wanted to increase your income you had to work more hours or find a way to get paid more money per hour. It felt like a revelation to learn that some people earned income in a passive manner that did not depend on the number of hours they worked.

I learned in the book about the power of passive rental income that I could earn by acquiring properties and renting them to tenants. I immediately scratched this option off my mental list. By this point in my life, I did not have any extra money and my credit score was terrible. Another example was building a book of business as an insurance professional. I learned that insurance professionals earned a commission when they signed up a new customer and that they earned passive income when the customer continued to pay for an insurance policy. Building a book of business in insurance would allow me to create passive income that would continue to come in.

The lessons in the book dominated my thoughts. There were also challenges preventing me from getting started as an insurance professional. First, I could not afford to quit my job while learning the life insurance business, and I could not find a company interested in hiring me on a part-time basis. Second, I would have to study for and pass an exam to become licensed to sell insurance. Third, and most problematic for me, was that I had no real-world sales experience. Delivering furniture and working retail jobs had not prepared me for professional sales and I was unsure that I could become a polished sales professional myself.

My frustration grew as I searched for a new job immediately and at the same time I remained excited for the potential of finding a way to begin earning passive income. In my search, I came across an opportunity I was not expecting. A product that I already owned and loved. I had never considered selling it until that moment. I had told many people about it over the years but I was never paid for those referrals. Although I did not realize it at the time, my life would never be the same.

I remember staring at that screen and feeling excited about what I had just found. I also remember going over the information again and again looking for the catch. Was it possible that I could earn a significant commission for selling a product that I was so familiar with and happy with myself? On top of that, I would also be able to continue earning passive income every month when the customer reordered. It was almost too good to be true. I had just found the answer to my searches.

Not only was I going to be able to sell this product and earn an income, but I was also going to be able to recruit other people to do so as well. Now my dream opportunity with ongoing passive income just became even bigger in my mind. I could build a team. I could build distribution. I could have leverage.

I immediately thought about all the people I worked with that were dissatisfied and everyone I knew that needed an additional stream of income. It was the first of many nights I would lie awake calculating the ways to leverage this business opportunity in order to change my financial future. I did not have a college degree, nor did I need one. I would not have to quit my job because I could start my new business part-time. As a customer already, I felt that the product was definitely better than advertised. Even though this business could potentially be worth millions of dollars to me, it would not cost tens of thousands of dollars as a franchise would.

The initial investment would be less than three hundred dollars to start my business.

At the time, I did not have an extra three hundred dollars. That was a substantial sum of money to me. I could not just write a check or put it on a credit card, but I was not going to let that stop me. In order to make the investment, I would have to make sacrifices. My finances were so tight that I chose to get further behind on my bills to start this business. The way I saw it, I could not afford to get started but I also could not afford to waste any more time. I needed to take action.

I started my direct sales business with a goal of earning $400 a week so I could quit my job and control my own schedule. I reached that income goal while continuing to work full time. Eventually, I left the world of traditional jobs behind and continued to increase my income. I was inspired and motivated by my mentors to set new goals. It was not long after I made this business my primary focus that I was able to earn over $100,000 per year. At the time of publication, I have earned over one million dollars in total income with my direct sales business. Even so, I believe that I am still at the beginning of what is possible. I also feel strongly that the most common reasons others do not have the same results can be overcome by applying the lessons I have learned on my journey.

My journey to success has been a radical one and my path has been characterized by resilience. Staying on this path and continuing to be resilient has not been easy, but it has been empowering.

The robbery was many years ago. It is not an easy story to recollect or share, but I share it because it marks the beginning of my journey. At that moment and the days that followed, I made a decision to take control of my life. The events that took place that night in Providence caused me to take action immediately that I may have continued putting off forever. If the robbery had not happened I would not have acted so quickly to take the needed steps to move in a new direction with my life.

Empowered Action

In this section, you are going to take inventory of your current financial situation while also creating a clear vision for your financial future. If you have a spouse do this activity together.

To begin, write down all the debt you would like to pay off. Would a new income stream allow you to pay off credit cards, student loans, or other lingering bills? If so, write them down. If you are one of the majority of people that feel trapped by debt you can actively release yourself from these burdens by prioritizing paying off your debts with the income from your direct sales business.

The first step is to make a complete list of every debt you owe and the total amount owed. Write down exactly how much more money you will have per month when you are no longer servicing these debts.

Once your list is complete write a clear statement on how your life will be different when these debts are paid off. Write down how it feels to be completely debt-free. Write this in the present tense. For example, "I am debt free and I feel like a weight has been taken off my shoulders."

What about your retirement goals? Because of the burden of lingering debt, most people are not able to sufficiently fund their future retirement which often leads to delaying retirement. If you want to be able to retire in the future you can fund your retirement plans with the income from your direct sales business. Write down on your list exactly when you want to retire, how long you plan to live after you retire and how much money you will need to live in those years after retirement. Write down how much money you currently have saved for your retirement. This is simple math, if you are not going to have enough money to retire when you plan to you need to find ways to increase your income now. It is important to have a clearly written goal of when you want to retire and not live day to day with no plans for the future.

Do you have children or grandchildren? Most people would love to do more for the current and future needs of their children and grandchildren. Write down all the ways you would like to financially support these important young people in your life. Would you like to fund a college savings account? Are these children in the very best public school system or would moving to a new city or at least transferring to private school help them to have the best education? Are these children missing out on opportunities in sports, the arts, or special academic programs simply because the costs are prohibitive for your family?

Do you want the best for yourself, your spouse and your family? You can provide a new home in a safer neighborhood, more reliable vehicles, healthy organic food, the best supplements and medical care, and great vacation memories for your whole family by creating additional income from a direct sales business. If any, or all of these are important to you write them down on your list as well.

I have heard many people tell me that they do not need any extra income in their families with great confidence. Once they complete their list, they realize just how many more opportunities are available to them and the motivation to create additional income becomes clear.

Empowered Conclusion

You do not need more jobs, you need a source of passive income. If you have a job already, that is not a reason to dismiss the power of building a direct sales business in your spare time. You might miss out on the opportunity to get started because you see the world as black and white. This represents a type of cognitive distortion, polarized thinking. "If you already have a source of income you do not need another." Seeing things only in extremes causes one to miss out on opportunities that others seize.

Having a job should not mean that an additional source of income for your household is unwelcome. I do not imagine that you would directly turn down the ability to qualify for free vacations or opportunities to travel the world. I would be surprised if you felt like you had all the time freedom you could ever need. While you may want the benefits of a successful direct sales business, your black and white thinking does not allow you to see the powerful opportunities that you may be passing up.

Empowered Thoughts

"I am building a powerful direct sales business because it allows me the freedom to make choices that are important to me."

"The world is abundant with opportunity. I intentionally attract this abundance to me every day."

Your Empowered Affirmation

In the space that follows, develop a personal, strength-based affirmation to combat your negative thinking about seizing opportunities.

Jim Tanner

Distortion 2: I Do Not Like Sales

"If you don't like something, change it. If you
can't change it, change your attitude."
– Maya Angelou

I left high school with my life all figured out. I
had no interest in going to college because it
would just slow down my plans. I was going to
be an athlete and an entertainer. I had a dream to
see the world and be rich, but less than a year
after I graduated I found myself back in
Whitehall, New York where I had finished high
school. I was delivering furniture and wondering
how things could have gone so wrong. What had
felt like a dead-end delivery job actually ended up
opening the door to my entire future.

It was at this job on my lunch break when a man
walked into the store and asked if he could show
me something. He said it would only take fifteen
minutes. He also said I may or may not be
interested. A decade later I would learn that
those three sentences were exactly how to invite
someone to sit down for a product
demonstration in our company. At this moment
he was just a salesman and I was just a guy on his
lunch break. Fifteen minutes later I was writing
him a check and becoming a new customer. I
was impressed by the product and what it had to

offer. I never saw that man again after that day but he gave me access to a product that I was very satisfied with and ten years later I would start my own business marketing this same product. Over the course of those ten years, I used the product and got great value from using it to the point that I would tell other people about my results as a customer.

Most, if not all, people in direct sales would say that they believe in their product. When I am coaching someone that is not having success in direct sales, I usually discover the reason for their lack of success very quickly. They do not actually *believe* in the product at all. They mistake belief for hope. They *hope* for the quality and viability of the product, but they do not believe it. It is important to recognize the difference between hope and belief.

When you are just getting started in your business, you have recently been introduced to an incredible product and are excited about it. You may actually know very little about the product at this point. You hope that it works as advertised and you hope that the things you are learning about the product are true. You hear testimonies about how the product has helped other people and you secretly wonder if those are real people sharing their genuine results. When I spend time talking to people about their frustrations it becomes clear that they are not using the products they sell on a regular basis. This will definitely lead to struggle and frustration early on.

You may become frustrated particularly if you have been recruited into the business by promises of fast money with very little effort. Companies and leaders may say that your enthusiasm is more important than your knowledge and you do not need to get caught up in the details. However, in my opinion, this messaging is too broad. While you may not need to know every detail of your product to be successful, you do need to be a real believer in the products and the results that come from using them correctly.

The potential customers you meet with do not need to borrow your hope. Your customers need to borrow your belief. If you have not established a belief in your products, people will not buy your product or join your team. This is not unique to direct sales but is true of every form of sales. Selling is the transfer of emotion from you to the customer. You are transferring everything you feel about the product. Are you transferring your conviction or your uncertainty? Are you transferring your passion or your unease?

When I started my business I had a tremendous advantage. Every time I sat down with a prospect to present the product, I radiated genuine belief because I was already a long-time customer. I was armed with countless personal stories about successfully using the product. My customers were able to borrow my belief rooted in genuine positive feelings which were generated by my actual experiences and results. The prospect could feel my passion and because of that passion, many of them wanted to buy.

Additionally, my steadfast confidence in the product served to protect me from the rejection I faced from some prospects, including close friends and family. Not everyone would buy. Some people would not even schedule a time to meet with me. Had I not believed in my product, I would have become greatly discouraged and assumed that these prospects saw a flaw in the product that I had somehow missed. Instead, because of my personal experience as a customer, I was protected.

Many people that should start a direct sales business do not because they think that they cannot succeed in sales. This cognitive distortion is known as emotional reasoning. Emotional reasoning is the false belief that your emotions are the truth — that the way you feel about a situation is a reliable indicator of reality. If these people look deeper they would realize that direct sales is a word of mouth marketing business model. Success does not come from mastering a sales script, overcoming objections, or other techniques of a sales transaction. Success comes when you share your story about the product you are representing. You share how you have personally gotten results that are meaningful to you. I do not see that as sales, I see it as educating. I am educating people that my products exist and telling true stories of how they have helped me and other people.

Unfortunately, many people that do get started quit very early on in their direct sales business because of a little rejection. A negative reaction from a prospect creates doubt in the mind of a new distributor because that new distributor has not yet established a strong belief in the product and does not understand their role as an educator. They see themselves in a sales role and thus when someone does not buy from them right away they label that interaction as a failure and they predict that all of the future interactions will have the same result. In cognitive distortions, this is known as mental filtering. This is a tendency to ignore positives and focus exclusively on the negatives.

As a business owner in direct sales, it is fundamental for you to own your product and use your product. Invest time in learning about how it works and why it is better than other competing products in the marketplace.

What if you have a negative experience with the product? If this is the case you need to ask your mentors questions about why it did not work the way you thought it would. Perhaps your expectations are not aligned with reality. Realize that many direct sales businesses are bringing something new and revolutionary to the market. It may not be meeting your expectations at first but that does not mean it is not potentially great. You have to use your critical thinking skills to decide if you have a product that is real and valuable to the marketplace, being offered at a fair price. If so, you do not have to be a sales master to gain customers. Your personal experiences told as compelling stories is all that is needed.

Over the years I have noticed a certain phenomenon. When someone in my organization suddenly begins making sales and recruiting, sometimes after months or years of dormancy, more often than not, the reason they were inspired to action was that they realized how truly wonderful the product was and became excited to share it with others. In that excitement, the cognitive distortion was overcome. They were not imagining the negative outcome anymore. They have a product that brings them a benefit and they enjoy sharing it with others.

The cognitive distortion known as mislabeling is an extreme form of overgeneralizing. You may have tried a sales role in the past. You may not have had the success you expected immediately. Instead of seeing this as a natural part of the learning and growing process, someone suffering from this cognitive distortion may decide they are a failure and extend that out to say that they are not good at sales, creating for themselves a false belief that they carry forward with them in life. Mislabeling involves describing an event with language that is highly colored and emotionally loaded.

Empowered Action

You are going to take inventory of your personal experience as a customer of your product. You are also going to use critical thinking to determine if success in your direct sales business actually requires selling skills.

Make a list of every product that you personally use from your company. It may be only one product or it could be many products, make sure it is a complete list. For each product on your list write down a direct benefit that you have experienced personally. For example, It may be that you have more energy, lost five pounds, gained strength, sleep better, save money, etc. For each product on your list write down if you plan to continue using the product and for how long. For every product on your list that you believe you will continue to use in the future write down why you will continue to use it in the future. Write down for each product if you believe that other people would have similar positive experiences using the product.

Make a list of five things you have recommended to someone that is not produced by your company and that you were not paid a commission for referring. It could be products you love, restaurants you enjoyed, movies you watched, etc. You should be able to easily think of five and some can make a list of many more.

The point of making these lists is to help you visually see where your direct sales business fits into the world you already inhabit. Direct sales is not the same as traditional selling where you have to overcome objections and master a closing script. Direct sales is word-of-mouth marketing. It is simply the act of sharing your personal story of using and loving a product with other people that you also believe would get a similar benefit.

Empowered Conclusion

You do not need to love sales to build a direct sales business. I have seen time and time again people with massive amounts of sales experience struggle, get frustrated, and quit. I have also seen teachers, pastors, retail workers, stay at home parents, factory workers, nurses, military veterans and a host of other people with no sales skills join our profession and thrive. The deciding factor is not sales skills or the ability to master a sales process. The people that succeed in direct sales use the product, realize a benefit from using it, and enjoy sharing their results so that others can discover the product and gain a benefit as well.

Empowered Thoughts

"I radiate belief in my product and I am grateful for the ways it has helped me."

"I already have the skills I need to educate others about the benefits of my product."

Your Empowered Affirmation

In the space that follows, develop a personal, strength-based affirmation to combat your negative thinking about sharing your product.

Distortion 3: You Have to Get in Early

"You never know how or when you'll have an impact, or how important your example can be to someone else."
– Denzel Washington

Tears rolled down my face uncontrollably. I was sitting in the second row of seats on the aisle at the Grand Ole Opry in Nashville, Tennessee. I am not known for my public displays of emotion and this one caught me off guard. I hoped no one would notice but as I was trying to collect myself I felt two hands on my shoulders from behind. They were the strong hands of one of my friends in the company. As he gave me a squeeze he whispered words of understanding. He had experienced the same thing many times and knew exactly what I was feeling. Suddenly, I was fine with the tears and I let them flow freely.

The moment on that stage that I was reacting to was my friends, Adam and Allicia Thompson, speaking to the thousands in attendance. They were on the stage being recognized for reaching a significant milestone in their business. They are part of our organization, but they are also our friends. I have had the pleasure of watching them build their business from the start. They have a successful business and they are also the most gracious and generous humans I have ever met. On that day in Nashville, Adam and Allicia spoke from the heart about what their business has enabled them to provide for their family, friends, and community. It was emotional for me and it was emotional for everyone in attendance. They are two of the most honest, hard-working, and dependable people you could ever meet. When they started their direct sales business, the company had already been in business for decades.

The company I joined at twenty-eight years old had been in business since before I was born. While I was living my life the company was growing, improving its product, refining its compensation plan, and expanding into more states and countries. While I was in a season of my own preparation the company became a vehicle for many people to earn extra income, change careers, and gain freedom. When it was my time to join the company, it had already stood the test of time and been proven in many ways.

I am grateful for the pioneers that built the company I would eventually join. Early adoption actually has nothing to do with your chances of success. This is a myth perpetuated by the smoke-and-mirrors direct sales startups with questionable products, shaky financials, and more hype than substance. When I joined my company I was told by others that I was getting in too late. It is easy to get discouraged by people that you care about who may say something like this to you. You just have to understand, like I did, that they do not have the facts. Knowing the facts is so critical to your ability to stay focused.

By the time I first heard someone suggest to me that my business was a "pyramid scheme," I had already stood in an arena and listened to Governors, Attorneys General, and other elected officials that recognize the efforts of our company and the distributors. They certainly were not going to appear on stage in front of thousands of people to speak on behalf of an illegal business. Unfortunately, for many people that start their business, all it takes is one of these thoughtless statements from a well-meaning and uneducated friend or family member to make them reconsider pursuing their new dream of financial freedom.

Getting into your direct sales business before someone else does not guarantee more money or success. I have known distributors that earned a few thousand a month with their business but had people in their team that earned six figures per year. In my own team, while I got started before the other distributors I recruited, I was not the first person in my team to earn $100,000 in a single year. I was not the first to earn a multiple six-figure annual income and I was not the first to earn over a million dollars in total income.

In a real direct sales business, the majority of the income goes to the top producers, not the people that happened to join before the top producers. I find this to be fair and just. When I learned about this aspect of direct sales it reminded me immediately of my favorite job in high school, working at a wild animal park in the Lake George region of New York.

Today, the ten-acre "Lake George Zoo" is gone. Where it once stood is now an overflow parking lot for the amusement park across the road. Back then it was the place where I learned a lot about hard work and got a pretty solid understanding of how to face fears and get out of my comfort zone. The rules were strict: protect the animals, employees, and visitors.

While most of my high school peers mowed lawns or worked at an ice cream shop, I was spending my days with bears, lions, kangaroos, zebras, tigers, reptiles, and monkeys. Before working at the zoo, I had washed dishes at one restaurant, been a waiter at another, and worked at a grocery store.

Working at the zoo was different. It was the first time that I could clearly see working harder than everyone else made a difference. I had never avoided hard work. I had countless examples within my family of how working hard mattered. The man that gave me the job was in charge of the entire property. He was responsible for the land, the animals, the employees, and the guests. He was a serious man that valued hard work as well as respect for the potential dangers of working near these unpredictable animals. Employees were let go for being late, missing shifts, or for being unsafe around the animals.

I loved the structure and the high expectations of this job. I worked hard and my boss noticed. I was given more responsibilities and more hours. I worked every day after school and all summer. I loved working hard and being outdoors, but more than anything I loved the fairness of having my hard work rewarded. I had not experienced that in my previous jobs.

When my time at the zoo was done and I had to move on, I was often frustrated that instead of being recognized for my hard work, it was overlooked. The best hours, shifts, and jobs would go to the person who had been there the longest or was friends with the right people. Outworking everyone else was not valued. I missed the simpler times at the zoo. It would be many years before I was again in an environment where I was recognized for the work I was doing.

When I entered the profession of direct sales it reminded me of working at the zoo a decade earlier. It did not matter who was in the company the longest. It was irrelevant who was friends with who. The opportunity to earn more income and get promoted through the compensation plan was available to everyone. The fairness I had been seeking from traditional jobs had been waiting for me in the profession of direct sales.

It is not the people that get in early that make the most money in direct sales. The people that have realized the most success have produced the most and served their customers and team in the most meaningful ways. Most people work hard for a job that pays them a wage for their time and effort. Too often, working hard and doing quality work is not nearly as valued as having been with the company the longest. Who you know can be more important than what you produce. Getting in early is an advantage in a traditional career in the corporate world, but does not provide an advantage in the profession of direct sales.

An advantage of a direct sales business that is often overlooked is the ability to create generational wealth. Building a team of distributors allows you to earn income from other people's production. This is only part of the potential. Every customer that you and your team acquire has the potential to increase your passive income as that happy customer reorders or adds other products from your catalog now and into the future. This is not generational income, however. That customer will eventually stop ordering or die. passive income is not perpetual, because customers do not live forever.

If you build a team of people that acquire new customers and new distributors, you have a machine that can create generational wealth. Every day new customers come into the fold and, more important, new distributors join the business and add more customers and distributors. That is geometric growth. When you have a business with leaders that are driving the right behaviors, you have a business that can last longer than you. This is why I believe that direct sales is the perfect business model. You can start without risk, with little capital investment and virtually no skills, and build a passive income now and for generations of your family in the future.

Passive income is income that continues to be realized by you in the future but is no longer dependent purely on your time. For example, before direct sales, I earned income from an employer by trading my time for their dollars. When I stopped giving them my time they stopped giving me their dollars.

Passive income can come in many forms: royalties from book sales, licensing fees for an invention that you own the patent on, rents from real estate that you own, dividends from investments, etc. In direct sales, passive income usually comes in the form of commissions from customers reordering your products every month, and if you build a team, it comes in the form of income paid to you from the sales being produced by your distributors.

Most people live their entire lives without realizing that passive income is available to them. Unfortunately, it is not as visible to the average person as linear income and so it is easy to miss the opportunities that create passive income. There are three major factors that prevent most people from having passive income and if you personally do not know anyone that has passive income this will help you to understand why.

First, it is hard to create passive income. That will take most people out right there. It is human nature to avoid pain. In modern times that usually means staying in our comfort zone.

Second, there is a time delay built into passive income. People that are not knocked out by the difficulty are usually crushed by the time delay. We are conditioned for instant results. If we work eight hours today we want to get paid for eight hours today. We are taught that any alternative is a scam and must be avoided at all costs. The book you are reading tells stories that took me forty-three years to live and five years to write in my spare time. It took weeks to edit. After investing that time and attention, this project will provide my family with passive income from every book sold. Most people will not take the time to write a book today for income that will be realized sometime in the future.

Third, there is an investment. Society suggests that the requirement of investment is also a sign of a scam. This advice is pervasive. The investment is not always money, sometimes it is time. If you write a book or create an invention you are going to invest time. If you buy a franchise or develop an apartment complex you are going to invest money and time. In the direct sales model, we invest a little money upfront to get started. Usually a few hundred dollars. This often filters out people that should start the business but do not because they have a negative bias about making an investment.

If you want to develop passive income you will need to invest time and money in the beginning. If you are working for someone else on an hourly or annual salary, you are working for someone that invested time and money to develop passive income for their present and future. You are being leveraged as a part of their passive income plan. There is nothing wrong with that. If you understand passive income and you are fine with being the person to provide it for your boss and the shareholders, continue doing what you have been doing. If you want that passive income for yourself, recognize that it does not come from being in a position of an hourly or salary employee. You will need a vehicle like direct sales to create that passive income stream.

Empowered Action

In this exercise, you are going to gather some facts and write them down. This information is important to your understanding of your company and the potential of the opportunity. You may not already know the answers to these questions but you will be able to find them with the help of your company website and your sponsor.

Start by gathering information about your company. When did your company launch? It could have been very recently and it could have been decades ago. Write down the year that your company began operations. Next, write down why your company was formed and launched. What is your company's story? It is important to understand the motivation behind your company and the founder's decision to create the company you are aligning with to build your business.

Finally, is your company publicly traded or privately held? Make sure you have the answers to these questions written down.

Next on your list is information about your products. Every company has a product that defines it, we call this a flagship product. What is the flagship product of your company? Approximately how many people already use your company's flagship product? List the countries around the world where your company's flagship product is available. Finally, how does your company's flagship product improve on similar products already available? It could be price, ingredient quality, customer service, or many other factors that give your company's flagship product an advantage over other products in the marketplace.

Now that you have completed this exercise reflect back on what you have learned. Whether you have a new company or an established company there will be advantages and disadvantages. A new company brings the excitement of a startup but lacks the testimonials of successful distributors and happy customers. A company that has been around a long time may not have the same startup energy but instead has a lot of testimonials from happy customers and success stories from proven leaders. The purpose of this exercise is to help you understand that you are part of a real company with real products that set out to solve a real problem in the marketplace. When your company launched, or when you joined is not nearly as important as why your company exists and why you are participating in the business yourself.

Empowered Conclusion

Success in direct sales is not dependent upon getting in early. In reality, getting in early is not valued in direct sales like it is in traditional corporate careers. Doing the simple activities that lead to success is valued because these activities lead to results. In direct sales, results are rewarded. There are no politics, no emphasis on tenure or other factors that matter. The direct sales professionals that have had the most financial reward have achieved these results by executing the daily simple activities that lead to success. Some have done it faster than others for a variety of reasons but none have achieved success because they got in first.

Believing that success is only for those who get in early is a fallacy in thinking. This type of thinking represents a distortion in our thoughts about fairness and our capacity for control. If you do not address this way of thinking, you may be prone to resentment or hopelessness. Instead, we must have a mindset of abundance. In reality, direct sales will provide opportunity and capacity for success; this opportunity is in direct relation to the action you are willing to take. You are in control of your outcome and capacity for success.

Empowered Thoughts

"I am open and ready to attract abundance into my life."

"I am having success in my business because my efforts are rewarded."

Your Empowered Affirmation

In the space that follows, develop a personal, strength-based affirmation to combat your negative thinking about abundance.

Jim Tanner

Distortion 4: I Do Not Have Time to Build a Business

"I alone cannot change the world, but I can cast
a stone across the waters to create many ripples."
– Mother Teresa

Total silence. I had played out the scene in my
mind over and over the previous nine months
but I never imagined this. The room was totally
silent and we were alone. Only moments before,
the room was so full of people that I wondered
where to stand. It was a choreographed dance of
medical professionals doing their job while my
wife gave birth to our daughter. I had silently
worried for nine months that this day would not
come, but as I held her tiny blanket-wrapped
body in my hands I had a new worry that I had
not considered prior. I feared that I was in the all
too familiar setting of losing one of the
important women in my life. . . this time my wife.

The birth had gone smoothly but immediately
after complications arose. I could feel the energy
shift in the room as all of these professionals said
reassuring things but acted with a sense of
urgency and emergency that was not in the air
before now. Finally, the doctor made the
decision it seemed he wanted to avoid. . . they
were taking Danielle to surgery. Nurses wheeled

my wife out of the room and all of the staff followed behind. Leaving just the two of us in an empty hospital delivery room. I watched our daughter blink her eyes and fall in and out of sleep in her first moments while I held her. I was grateful she was here and healthy but I was also deeply afraid of what might happen next.

Strong women have informed my most important decisions and guided my entire life. It began with my great grandmother Anna, who came from Italy to America through Ellis Island at nine years old. She grew up in Vermont, learned English, and eventually raised a family which included my grandmother. My grandmother raised her own family only a few miles away in the marble quarry town of Proctor, Vermont. She had four boys and one girl. That girl was my mother.

Many years later, I met the woman who would become my wife. Danielle clearly had the best qualities of each of the important women in my life. The moment I met her I knew I did not want to live my life without her. When I met her mother, the woman that would later become my mother-in-law, I marveled at how similar to my own maternal role models she was.

As surely as these women were delivered into my life to shape who I would become, eventually, age and illness began to take them away from me.

It started with my great grandmother. I was still young when she moved into a nursing home where she would live only a few more months. Alzheimer's robbed her ability to live in her own home, recall her favorite things, or look forward to the future. She had lived a full life and raised a first-generation American family. Her legacy of kindness and generosity lives on in the stories we tell today to her great-great-grandchildren. It is the first loss that I remember but it certainly would not be the last.

Many years later I was at the Charlotte airport waiting for a flight back home to Boston when my wife called to tell me that my grandmother was in the hospital. I told Danielle once my flight landed in Boston I would grab some clothes and drive the three and a half hours up to Vermont to the hospital. I didn't realize that I would be spending the next three weeks at that Vermont hospital. The next time I slept in my own bed at home would be the evening after my grandmother's funeral.

Only a few months after her funeral I got a call from my uncle. He asked if I thought anything was out of the ordinary with my mother. She had not been showing up at work. This was certainly alarming. My mother did not miss work. She had many sicknesses and plenty of challenges but she always showed up for work. Her co-workers were her friends and in our town the people that could land the well-paying jobs at a factory were grateful. She had been there for decades and was nearing retirement age. She would not simply stop going to work.

With the help of her doctors, we learned that she had been suffering from the symptoms of early-onset dementia. Many years before, she bought a small house for herself with a lot of land and very few neighbors. She loved her privacy. When she was not at work she spent her free time tending her flowers and living a quiet life. Over time she had stopped working in her gardens and maintaining her home. She had neglected to pay bills and keep groceries in the house. She was not regularly eating or bathing.

It was not safe for her to continue working and she was forced to retire. It had also become unsafe for her to drive and both her car and license were taken from her. Once her oasis of privacy, her secluded home in Vermont was now a danger to her. I had hoped she could continue living at home with visiting nurses but it was soon apparent that she would need full-time care. I had to be the one to move her from her beloved home to an assisted living facility. She argued a little but mostly cried.

My mother's childhood ended without warning. She overcame violence, sadness, loneliness, and loss. She was the most independent person I have ever known and now that was being taken away from her too. For what was left of her life she would be totally dependent on others. The disease is vicious. It takes the person you love; their personality, their traits, their habits, and their memories, but leaves behind the physical body for months or years to continue to remind you of just how much you have lost.

One by one the women vanished. My wife was nine months pregnant with our daughter when we gathered in the cemetery at our family plot to mourn the passing of my mother-in-law. What had started out as some pain the prior summer was cancer. By spring we were saying goodbye. After a celebrated career as a nurse, her instinct for taking care of everyone was legendary. When someone was sick she brought them food. When relatives got older she looked after them. When you needed help she knew even if you did not ask. She was by all accounts tremendous. Her passing left a void that was impossible to fill. She had taken care of her home, her family, members of her community, and more.

I was worried about my wife during this time. I worried about our baby. We had many challenges in getting pregnant. We had twice suffered the devastation of losing a pregnancy and I was worried that the stress and emotion of losing her mother would lead to this brutally familiar end once again. The pain of all of those memories was on my mind when I held my tiny daughter in my hands in that silent delivery room. Suddenly the silence was broken as a nurse returned to transfer us into our hospital room. She told me that Danielle was already in the room. At the last moment, the surgery was not needed after all. She was waiting for us. I took a breath, stood up, and followed the nurse anxious to reconnect with my wife and bring her our daughter.

***

People often say the reason they are not interested in starting a direct sales business is that they do not have time. They think of the people and activities that they already struggle to allocate attention and time to in their lives and they do not want to create further challenges when it comes to making time for the people that matter most to them. In the time I have been building my business, my country has seen record high and record low employment. Throughout it all, the need for a life plan that includes creating passive income streams remains.

A successful direct sales business creates the freedom to make choices. This freedom has been invaluable when it comes to life, health, and even death in my family. Our profession is over-represented by sports cars, boats, big houses, and so on that illustrate the lifestyle you can have with a successful direct sales business. When I think about the lifestyle I do not think about fancy cars. I think about three weeks sitting at my grandmother's bedside in a hospital without asking anyone for time off or explaining to anyone why I am not coming in to work. I think about a life without worrying about how I am going to pay my bills if I do not go back to work.

I have a big family and over the course of those three weeks aunts, uncles, cousins and other relatives and friends came and went. Those from out of town wondered if they should stay another day or go back home and go to work. They asked me for my opinion on if they should stay or go and come back later. That scene played out over and over again, all day every day during those three weeks. People checked with their employers to see if they needed to use vacation time. I did not have to do any of that. For three weeks I woke up every morning and went over to the hospital. Without asking anyone for permission, I did this every day until my grandmother passed. I think about the challenges of meeting with lawyers, doctors, home health aides, and others while trying to manage my mother's transition into care. I think about the time and effort it took to try to fill the gaps as family members and friends struggle with health, life, and death.

During the early days of the Covid-19 pandemic when there seemed to be more questions than answers, my direct sales business again gave me choices that other people simply did not have. I did not have to go out to work and potentially expose myself and I did not have to wonder if I was bringing a dangerous virus home to my family. I could stay home and continue to build my business.

To me, the lifestyle of a direct sales professional means freedom to control your choices, your schedule, and your income. You can leverage that for a luxury lifestyle but there will be many important moments you may have never considered that will make you grateful for that freedom as well.

Of course, there is a lot of fun to be had, and I would not want to gloss over the experiences my family has had since being involved with our direct sales company. Growing up, I had not gone anywhere or seen anything beyond my small-town life. I saw the world through television shows and magazines. I do not recall leaving the state many times at all in my childhood. That created a desire in me to want to see the world, but I honestly did not know how I was going to make that happen. Aligning with my company and this powerful profession allowed me to see the world, and more importantly, allowed me to show my daughter the world now instead of someday in the future. I went on an airplane for the first time in my twenties and got my passport in my thirties. My daughter had traveled by plane two dozen times before she was two years old and had her passport before her first birthday.

I have walked the beaches of the world with my wife and daughter and that is pretty cool. We have been joined on those beaches by some of the most successful business builders in our profession, which is an incredible bonus. The best part though is that it is all provided by the company at no cost to us in the form of incentive trips that we can qualify for throughout the year. I have prioritized qualifying for these trips and experiences over the last several years and it has been very rewarding.

A few years ago, we traveled to Iceland and witnessed the Northern Lights, rode snowmobiles across a glacier and drove Land Rovers across volcanic fields. We ate great, local food and had amazing conversations. This is a scene that repeats itself over and over. We have eaten the best foods, had the best experiences and conversations in places like Cabo, Jamaica, Bahamas, and Cancun. All-inclusive, all expenses paid, and always above expectations. We have experienced private shows in Las Vegas and exclusive access to theme parks. Watching my family and friends experience VIP treatment has been a lot of fun and I am looking forward to the memories we will continue to create on these adventures.

How you choose to spend your time, money, and opportunities in life is up to you. I know that a successful direct sales business can give more choices. When someone asks me if building this type of business is worth the time and energy I can answer with an emphatic "YES", because I know how many additional options and opportunities became available because of direct sales. It has not all been about luxury for our family. It is the freedom to control our own life that makes this a lifestyle worth pursuing. Some of the best examples come from ordinary everyday things that you may never notice unless you are looking for them.

I recall watching a young boy scan the crowd. One of my daughter's classmates at school. We were at the spring assembly and I immediately picked up on this boy stretching his neck around from his seat up front looking back at the audience. It was so familiar to me and I knew exactly what he was doing. He was looking for someone. Maybe it was his mom or dad. Maybe a grandparent or some other adult that was important in his life. He wanted to see if they had arrived. I recognized this because I had been that boy myself. I was the one looking out from the school assembly, the play, the baseball game for someone in my family to be there watching.

There had been a few times when I scanned the audience, recognized someone, and felt that excitement, but more often than not, in my school career, the families in the audience would not include mine.

I told my wife about this scene as we walked back to the car. She had not noticed the boy herself. I described the feeling of familiarity and I could tell that she could not relate. She would tell you that her experience was the opposite. Home games or away, daytime or evening if there was an event, her family would be there. Her parents coached sports and volunteered at events. They were always able to be there for their children.

My approach to parenting in many ways represents the opposite of my experiences as a child. My wife approaches parenting as a way to duplicate her childhood experiences. Either way, our family wins because we are able to invest time and attention. We are able to be present in the moments that matter as well as the moments that we may not realize the significance of until much later.

I was not a father when I started my direct sales business. I was not married to my wife either. Over time the reasons I was building my business shifted. It started out as a way to give me more flexibility and to supplement my income. When I was about to get married I transitioned my part-time side business into my full-time career. When I became a dad I reimagined my business as a way to provide generational wealth to future members of my family. These adjustments in my areas of focus lead me to want, more than anything, to work with busy parents. I love to help parents build a business that allows them total agency, the agency that I have been able to experience through my business.

Many mornings I will watch interstate ninety east heading into Boston from the suburbs where I live. The parking lot of my gym gives me a great view of the scene below. Cars by the thousands in gridlock as they crawl the same road where only a few hours later cars will zip by at eighty miles an hour. I know some of those people love their jobs and do not suffer a moment of regret. I also know that in many of those vehicles the occupants are reluctantly driving away from the spouse and children that matter the most to them. Dads and moms that would love to be with their kids all day but do not know what other options exist. They have not heard of direct sales. They do not know that an alternative life exists where they are in total control of their finances and their schedule. Simple reminders appear to me daily that I live a charmed life.

When I bring my daughter to the playground I am typically the only dad. I am not the only dad that wants to play with his kid at the playground, I am just the dad that gets to do it during the week. On Saturday at the same playground, you will see all the dads. Perhaps to the rest of them, I am a Saturday playground dad as well. They would not know that I have been there all week long. The first two years of my daughter's scheduled pediatric doctor appointments are another great example. I remember her doctor telling us at the two-year appointment that he could not recall another time that both parents attended every office visit during the first two years. It was another reminder that not every parent gets to live this life.

The examples are seemingly endless. Going to the movies on a weekday afternoon with your child is very different from fighting crowds on Friday or Saturday night. The same could be said for the grocery store or any number of other errands that most families are forced to attend to after work or on the weekends. The lifestyle that is available to all of us as direct sales professionals constantly motivates me to share the story of my own company and opportunity. I know that I can help others create financial freedom that reflects what is most important to them.

Empowered Action

In this section, you are going to take inventory of the actual time that you have available every day. You will identify the time that will be protected each day known as your "empowered hour." Once you have a better understanding of how you use time on a daily basis, you will be able to determine where you can insert income-generating activities with your direct sales business.

Track everything you do in the day. The time you start, the time you finish. Be specific on exactly what you are doing, do not just write "work". This can be done in a phone calendar, or on paper. You may need to do multiple days if your activity differs from day to day.

Note the time that you wake up and the time you go to sleep. What are the activities that make up the time in between? Do you have a job? If you do, write down the time you are at work and make note of any travel time to and from your job as well. Take the time to capture everything. Do you make breakfast for your family? Do you wait outside with your children until the school bus picks them up?

Rate your energy level at each part of the day. This will help you identify when you are most productive and efficient. There may be more than one peek in energy, note that as well.

Identify spaces where you can get help. Can you recruit help from family for cleaning and household chores? Identify the activities in your day that are time-wasting like scrolling social media, watching television, etc.

Once you have a completed list check it again. Taking this inventory is going to help you find the time to build your direct sales business without compromising the needs of the people that are counting on you every day.

Now that you have your daily routine written down, look for one "empowered hour" that you can identify on a daily basis that you can fully devote to your business. Your "empowered hour" can be a single sixty-minute block of time, two thirty-minute blocks, or four fifteen-minute blocks. What matters is that you determine where that hour can be positioned in your day and that you are serious about focusing on your business during that time. While you are identifying this time also consider what time of day you feel the most energized and what time of day you feel tired and consider that when scheduling your business time.

Next, identify the activities that will lead to success in your business and use your "empowered hour" time to do these activities only. Some thoughts on the best business-building activities include adding prospects to your list of potential customers and distributors, inviting these individuals to learn more about your product and opportunity, and following up with people that you invited to learn more previously. These are business-building activities and in a few minutes, you can connect with multiple people by phone, text, online video, or other communication methods each day.

Finally, look for places in your schedule where you can grow personally and professionally. When can you listen to an audiobook, the replay of your team training call, or a great podcast? If you have a daily commute, are cleaning the house or picking up your child from practice, you can make a conscious choice to listen to information that will help you grow as an individual and a business owner without taking time away from your devoted business building or anything else that matters most.

By looking at your daily schedule and evaluating where income-producing activities can fit in you will have a better understanding of how you can wrap your life around your direct sales business. By looking critically at how you structure your average day and week you will start to see clear time periods where you can build your business.

Empowered Conclusion

People do have time to start a direct sales business, and it is critical to understand that a direct sales business does not take time away from the people and activities that are important to you, it provides a vehicle for you to gain more time.

You could forever change your life starting a direct sales business, or giving attention to a business you already started. People think they do not have time because their thinking is out of alignment. They engage in filtering, a type of cognitive distortion. Filtering means they take the negative and magnify those details while filtering out all positive aspects of a situation. They fail to see that you can build a business in your spare time.

An hour a day may not seem like it would yield any results but when you are doing the correct activities consistently over time the results begin to reveal themselves. Ultimately, you do have time to start a business. Sometimes you need to make time, by exploring those behaviors in your day that "waste" time. Intentional daily disciplines will allow you to grow your business, even with limited time. You need to change the way you think, and more importantly, address errors in thinking, in order to empower your path forward.

Empowered Thoughts

"I have time to build a successful direct sales business because success is not determined by the amount of time invested. Success is determined by the amount of focus given to my business in the time I have available."

"Time is abundant and the universe is rewarding my attention to my business by providing more opportunities to focus on the activities that matter most."

Your Empowered Affirmation

In the space that follows, develop a personal, strength-based affirmation to combat your negative thinking about time management.

Distortion 5: I Have Tried Before and It Does Not Work

"Our minds become magnetized with the dominating thoughts we hold in our minds and these magnets attract to us the forces, the people, the circumstances of life which harmonize with the nature of our dominating thoughts."
– Napoleon Hill

My entry into direct sales was not my first entrepreneurial experience. As a kid, I was always hustling – mowing lawns, washing cars, buying and selling things, and doing odd jobs. I wanted to have money in my pocket because from as far back as I could remember, every decision seemed to revolve around whether I could afford it.

I just hated being broke. I know my mom created a life for her son that was far better than what it might have been given the circumstances by which I came into this world. In order to achieve that, she worked in a factory. She had a good job with benefits. It was not glamorous, but it was the type of work that most people in small-town, rural Vermont coveted. As I was growing up, she always told me that I should shoot for more. Maybe she had that mother's instinct that I was destined for something different.

I had no interest in going to college. When the other kids were preparing for college I was trying to accumulate enough credits to get out of high school a year early. I would dream about a future where I was rich and traveled the world. I know my mom wanted me to achieve my dreams but I am sure she also worried about what my life would look like if I did not.

From a very young age, I tried a variety of different businesses. I had a table at my local flea market, started a sports entertainment company, and later when the internet emerged, I was buying and selling online. None of those early efforts yielded me any real results. If they had, I would not have been looking down the barrel of a gun that night in Providence.

I had tried and failed to be an entrepreneur over and over. I could have let the failures of the past define my future. Instead, I pushed forward with faith that the failures of the past did not mean I could not have success in the future. Direct sales allowed me to earn real money as an entrepreneur for the first time in my life. Unlike all the businesses I tried before, I quickly earned back my original investment and created a much needed additional income stream.

These lessons are not just limited to business. The first time I met my wife, I knew that very day that I would marry her and she would be in my life forever. There was no question in my mind. Her version of that first encounter was different because she assumed she would never see me again. Thankfully, I was right and she was wrong. We have been together ever since, and are partners in this business and in life.

When we met, we lived hours away from each other but later realized that we had been in the same town at the same time on several occasions. In fact, we had actually been in the same building at the same time. She had even met my mom long before we were introduced. It is possible that we could have never met. We could have missed each other dozens more times, like ships passing in the night. Eventually, a mutual friend introduced us and the rest, as they say, is history.

Prior to meeting Danielle, I had been in a few relationships that had ended poorly. I could have arrived at the mistaken conclusion that because those relationships had not worked out in the past, this one was doomed from the beginning. Thankfully, I did not give in to that thinking. Instead, I envisioned a brighter future for our relationship.

I had been reading the book *Think and Grow Rich* by Napoleon Hill and something about his lessons on definiteness of purpose spoke to me. I met Danielle shortly after I got specific and defined what I wanted my personal relationship with a life partner to be. That is why I knew right away that she was the one. I already had a clear image of what I wanted so I was prepared when the person I was looking for showed up in my life.

Growing up I lacked role models who were entrepreneurs. None of my family, close friends, or neighbors became successful by starting a business. Everyone in my life earned a living by working for someone else. There is nothing wrong with that. I have tremendous respect for hard work. I am forever grateful that the example of hard work was all around me in my formative years.

Danielle was raised with entrepreneurs in her family. Her grandfather Albie started a home heating oil company with no money. He took an incredible leap of faith and grew a thriving business from the ground up. At a time when people were literally lining up for work, he walked away from an offer of a steady job at the local mill because he knew it was not the road he wanted to travel. Everyone thought he was making a huge mistake. Albie recognized an opportunity where others saw scarcity and he did the hard work required to make it a success.

To this day his legacy as a businessman and a generous person continues to live on. I never got to meet him but I often ask my wife and father-in-law to tell me stories about him. Albie instilled in his family the understanding that anything is possible if you are willing to do the work. His entrepreneurial spirit helped to foster an environment of creative optimism for his descendants that lasts beyond the years of his own physical labor.

This example allowed Danielle to be incredibly supportive of my journey in direct sales, even in the earliest days. She had witnessed people in her family achieve business success. To her it was normal. It was not non-traditional. It was not unachievable. It was as simple as taking advantage of the opportunity and putting in the effort required to earn the desired results. This unwavering and optimistic support was critical to my future success. The best part was not simply having someone that believed in me, it was also the way Danielle inspired me to think bigger. Looking back with the benefit of hindsight, those moments I felt stuck in my business, in my relationships or in my life in general, were due to the fact that I was not thinking big enough.

It is common practice for us to remain in our comfort zone. Perhaps stretch it bigger ever so slightly a little at a time. It is not natural to set your sights on the top of the mountain. Before I started my business I was not surrounded by people that reached for huge financial accomplishments in the world. Most were just getting from one day to the next.

When you begin surrounding yourself with big thinkers, people that understand how the Universe actually works, it opens your mind to more possibilities. Could it be as simple as Napoleon Hill says? Can you just set your mind on a definite goal and everything falls into place to allow you to achieve it?

As a coach, if I can help someone set a definitive goal that they can clearly see, feel, and believe in, miracles will start happening for them in their business.

Unfortunately, most end up with no results and frustration because they are playing it small. I have been there. I wanted this business to pay me $400 a week so I could be in control of my own schedule. It did not occur to me that when I set that tiny goal to replace my current income I was still going to be broke all the time. I was broke at $400 a week from a job, why would it be different if I was making the same money from my own business?

That goal was definite in my mind and it did not take the universe long to line up the proper circumstances so I could achieve it but it did not solve anything. I did not have to become a different version of myself to earn that money. The miracle came when Danielle helped me to see that my goals were too small. We had a discussion about our present and our future. She helped me realize a goal that I could believe was possible since many others in the company had already done it but it was also way outside of my personal comfort zone. That goal was to earn $100,000 in a single year. When this goal became crystal clear in my mind it started to reveal a completely different road in front of me.

To achieve this, I was going to have to become a different person. I was going to need to read more, learn more, and become more than I was on the day I set the goal. I was going to need to get support from people that had already achieved that level of income which meant that I was going to be forced to interact with people that were outside of my comfort zone. I could no longer tell myself that my upline mentors were *"too busy"* or *"I do not want to bother them"* because if I was going to make this happen I needed their support. I was going to have to proclaim my goal to successful people that would hold me accountable to it.

Setting that definite goal improved my life. A short time later I was standing on stage being recognized for earning over $100,000 in a single year. I was a completely different person from the day I originally set the goal. I had gained a larger social circle of high achievers that I had met and worked with in pursuit of my goal. I had gained more customers and more team members than I ever had before.

Most importantly, I had proven to myself that I was capable of so much more than I had previously imagined.

I now understood the power of setting a definite goal and how much I would grow in pursuit of that goal if I was thinking bigger than I ever had before.

I hope when you read this, it inspires you to think bigger, to set a higher goal than you may be comfortable with right now. A goal that will cause you to stretch far beyond your comfort zone. A goal that will require you to work more closely with the high achievers in your company that had already reached and surpassed those goals and can help you design a path to get there as well.

In the past, I allowed myself to believe that the future could not be better. This distorted way of thinking represents an overgeneralization; I believed that since I had failed in the past, I would always fail in the future.

If I had not examined my distorted thinking around failure and success, I would never have started my business. Had I not started my business, I would not have been introduced by my mentors to personal development and self-improvement from people like Napoleon Hill. Had I not been reading those books I would not have gotten clarity on how I wanted to pursue a life and family. Without that clarity, I may never have met my wife.

Empowered Action

First, write down what would change for the positive by building a successful direct sales business. When you are making this list focus on finances, family, and service. Financial, identify what would change in your life financially. Write what you would be able to do with increased income. Family, what would change in your family's life? What ways can you imagine your family situation improving with a successful direct sales business? Service, what charitable causes could you support more robustly? What organizations or causes could you give more attention to if you have a successful direct sales business?

Next, write down the people that already believe in you and support you. This is not meant to be a list of people you think would be interested in your products or opportunity, this is a list of the people that cheer for you and celebrate you. Whether you started a pizza shop, a lawnmower repair business, or anything else they would be happy for you.

Start with family members. Your spouse, your children, siblings, or cousins? List the family members that want you to succeed. Once you have written down the family move to friends. Who are your friends that support you? Write them down. If you need inspiration look at your phone's message history and see who you communicate with the most. Do you have co-workers that believe in you? Make sure they are also on the list. How about members of your faith community? List those closest to you that you celebrate and mourn with during the happiest and saddest seasons of life. Again, write these names down so you can see who you feel supported by and how many people are on the list.

Finally, write down the people that you do not feel supported by. The categories are the same as above; family, friends, co-workers, and members of your faith community. Who do you worry would question you or make you question yourself if they found out that you were going to start a new business? It is just as important to take inventory of the people and relationships that you believe are holding you back as it is to list those that will cheer for you. Writing them down and acknowledging that these people exist in your world will give you power.

We all have supporters and detractors. Some of us have more of one than the other. You must decide to focus on the positive instead of wishing that the negative does not exist. You are in complete control and you have the power to choose to take action.

Empowered Conclusion

Giving yourself permission to dream again is not a frivolous time-wasting exercise. Dreaming and looking forward to a brighter future is the first step towards recognizing the opportunities being presented that will allow you to create that future.

Notice what you are telling yourself. Do not allow a cognitive distortion to hold you back from working toward improvement in your relationships, your health, your business, or your future.

Empowered Thoughts

"My past informs me but it does not define me. I carry forward the lessons from my life and I leave behind negative thoughts and emotions."

"My story matters, and I am still writing that story."

"I am resilient."

Your Empowered Affirmation

In the space that follows, develop a personal, strength-based affirmation to combat your negative thinking about success.

Jim Tanner

Distortion 6: It Was Easier for Them

"When I let go of what I am, I become what I
might be. When I let go of what I have, I receive
what I need." – Lao Tzu

When I turned sixteen all I could think of was
getting my driver's license and buying a car. I
imagined the freedom of the world opening up
around me. No more depending on others to get
around, I was about to be totally free. At sixteen
years old my mother gave birth to her first child,
me. She had to quit school and freedom was the
last thing on her horizon. It is difficult to imagine
what she dealt with. I sometimes wonder how
her family and friends reacted or how the news
must have spread quickly in such a small town. I
am sure that I would have been afraid. I was
thirty-eight when my daughter was born. I was
on a strong financial footing, I had a solid life
partner in my wife, an excited and supportive
faith community and family members that stood
ready to help. Even with all of that support, I
was still anxious, so I can only imagine what it
must have been like for my mother to learn that

her childhood was over and that she had disappointed so many people. The impact on her life of being a young mother would be felt over and over again. No college, no big-city career. She went to work at whatever jobs were available and finally got work at a factory in our town. A job she would keep for the next thirty years.

I am grateful for my mother and the life she provided. Under impossible circumstances, she did what she thought was right. We were not living on the streets. We had enough to eat, presents on holidays and always a place to call home.

Fortunately, we had a great family that acted as a safety net for my entire childhood. My grandmother was still raising her children when I arrived as her first grandchild. My uncles and grandfather stepped in and became my male role models. They were all great men, but could only provide limited influence on my life in the amount of time I was around them. I would mostly be exposed to them at family gatherings and holidays. My uncles grew up, started families, and lived as responsible men. Each of them today is a role model for their children and grandchildren.

I did not wish for my mother to be lonely but I did prefer it when it was just us. Unfortunately, as my mother dated, sometimes lived with, and even married men throughout the years she proved unable to select someone with the qualities of a role model that I could have benefited from during those formative years.

I grew up around alcoholism, violence, and drug abuse. My first memory of my mother being hurt was when I was five or six years old. In the moments after, when the violence subsided she made an effort to assure me that everything was going to be alright. It was my first memory of real danger but not my last.

Not long after, that same man threatened to kill us. He was driving and they were arguing. He raced the engine in the car and began driving at a high rate of speed while my mother begged for him to stop. She eventually left him and we moved into our own apartment the summer between my first and second grade school years.

For a few years, I remember life being fairly calm but when I was in fifth grade my mother moved her boyfriend into our apartment. He suffered from PTSD from his time in the Vietnam war. He would often scream out in his sleep. I was awakened countless times by the nightmares of this man sleeping in my mother's bedroom. Not long after meeting him, they bought a house together and we moved from that apartment.

I suppose my mother was willing to look past his anger, drinking, and mental challenges for a chance at her version of normal life and a family home. Unfortunately, our time in that home would be short. The summer before I started seventh grade he took his own life in the basement of that home. I was not there that night when my mother discovered his body. I can recall vividly being informed the next morning. My only emotion was relief. Not because he was gone but because my mother was safe. He was a dangerous man capable of hurting her or worse.

To settle his estate the house was sold. This caused my mother to move back home. The time I spent with my grandparents was a peaceful

oasis for me. No violence. No verbal abuse. I felt
safe but my mother nearly collapsed under the
emotional toll of these challenging days. She
abused alcohol and while she technically lived at
her parent's house with me, I did not see her
much. She was working third shift and I was
heading to school when she was coming back to
the house to sleep. Often, she was gone by the
time I got back from school.

I did spend some weekends and parts of my
summer vacations with my father. My father
eventually became a commercial truck driver but
when I was a kid he worked on dairy farms. At
that time, there were many dairy farms
throughout Vermont and upstate New
York. Some were small, some were large, and all
of them needed people to work the farm.

When imagining a dairy, you probably picture
Farmer John waking up early to milk his cow.
That may be what you read in storybooks but I
can assure you that the life of a dairy farmer is no
fairytale. Morning milking begins at four o'clock
in the morning, and that means waking up even
earlier to get the cows into the milking barn, get
them fed and milked. Many farms have hundreds

of nameless cows that are milked multiple times per day. My father's job was hard labor for which he was paid far too little.

Although my father worked for many different farms over the years, with a few exceptions, it was all the same. He would get up and work the morning milking and be back home for breakfast about the time that I was getting up. I would see him briefly while he ate and then he would go back out to the farm for the next round of responsibilities when the sun was up.

Depending on the time of year and the type of farm it could be just about anything. He mowed fields of oat, barley, and wheat to bale as hay for the animals to eat. A machine formed the bales and left them on the ground. My father collected these fifty-pound blocks from the field and stacked them on a hay wagon for transport to a storage barn. He lifted and stacked each of them for storage.

Some farms had a lot of equipment to make the job easier. Regardless of how much equipment was available on the farm, it was always hard work. It was hot in the summers and freezing in the winters. When he got a day off it was usually reserved for rest before returning to the brutal routine.

My father worked too hard for too little money and drank too much. Maybe drinking was how he dealt with feeling stuck in the cycle of his life. I wondered if he resented me. I certainly was not the product of a carefully planned family and I cannot imagine what he was feeling when he found out that my mother was pregnant. I doubt he wanted to stand in front of a preacher and get married to a sixteen-year-old girl while still in high school.

As I got older and gained more control over my own decisions about where I would go and when I saw a lot less of my father.

Overall, I could have done better to maintain contact but I did not feel motivated to do so. I reasoned that my father had a family of his own to look after. He was one of the many people who taught me by example how to work hard. For that, he deserves respect and admiration. I never heard him complain about getting up to do his job. He worked, brought home a paycheck to his family, and provided them a place to live. My father never rolled up in a ball and admitted defeat in desperate times. Instead, he rolled up his sleeves and got to work. I am glad I was able to learn from his example.

My mother did not like being back at her parents' house. She rented an apartment in town where it would be just the two of us. I liked living in Proctor, Vermont in those days. The town was small enough that you could get around on a bike or on foot. I could visit my grandparents anytime I wanted because they were so close. That said, I was still alone a lot.

When I was in ninth grade I remember not seeing my mother much. She still worked an overnight work schedule and days would sometimes go by before I would see her again. We communicated with each other by writing notes on a pad of paper. She would leave a note saying that she got groceries and I would leave a note in response. Years later when she was moved into a nursing home I cleaned out her house and I found a few of these notebooks. As I flipped through the pages and read the back and forth messages I was reminded of those days.

Once again, she moved a new boyfriend into our apartment, and shortly thereafter they bought a house together and it was time to move. My new home was about thirty miles away. I would not have the same freedom to walk or bike to my grandparents for dinner anymore. I started my tenth-grade year in a new school. This was my final time changing schools. In some ways, I was grateful to have a clean slate and a chance to make new friends that did not know every detail of my life like they did in the small town I had just left.

As I recall my past and relate it to my current business and team, I am constantly reminded that other people have not had an easier time. Often people struggling to build a direct sales business will assure themselves that others have had an easier time. They know that success is possible but they convince themselves that the people they see on stage had advantages they did not have. This represents a distortion in thinking. In reality, people have come from nearly impossible situations. Instead of allowing their past to determine their future, they utilize our profession as a vehicle to make a radical change in their life. Not because it was easy but because they could not imagine staying where they were and they took action.

Talented people find themselves paralyzed and intimidated by the process of letting go of the past. They often quit their new direct sales business before reaching their full potential. They seek out new products, leaders, and systems hoping something will be different. But wherever they go, whatever they do, they will inevitably reach the same closed door. Even if they change every aspect of their business, the one thing that will remain unchanged is the person they see in the mirror.

This is what I had to learn and what I work so hard to teach the people that I mentor:

1. You can do this.

I had to remind myself that I was capable, competent, and worthy. I realized that the evidence was on my side. Look at who has made it before you; read the stories. Learn about the people in direct sales who have succeeded: the challenges they faced, the uphill road they traveled, and their starting places. Despite it all, they succeeded.

Look at the stories of the people in your company who, with your products, your services, your leaders, and your compensation plan, excelled and improved their lives. Now they are paying it forward and acting as agents of change for many others.

When I began to think critically about the journeys of the most successful people I encountered in my company, it became clear to me that my own actions and motivation would be the key to my success or failure.

There are people at the very highest levels of the profession with less education, fewer advantages and opportunities, zero industry connections, and no family support. They made it with their own grit and determination. They were coachable and willing to do what was necessary. I realized there was no reason for me not to reach those levels and there is no reason why you cannot either.

2. Other people's opinions of you are irrelevant.

I used to take other people's opinions of me as fact. I let people tell me that direct sales does not work and that my company and my products do not make sense. I listened when the naysayers told me that other people could succeed, but not me. Many people in my life wondered why I could not just be happy delivering furniture. They wanted me to just go to work every day and accept my fate.

They were older than me and, I thought, wiser than me. I believe they had my best interest in mind, but if I had taken those opinions as fact, it would have been a disaster for my life. Instead, I chose not to absorb that negativity. By developing and maintaining belief in myself, I was able to change everything about my life and career.

Yes, It was challenging. I needed to develop many new skills, but that is true of any endeavor. I had to learn for myself not to limit either the scope of my vision or the number of people I could help.

Recognizing the negative influence of others as it happens allows you to choose your own path to success. It also gives you the opportunity to offer compassion to a friend or family member who is working through their own insecurities and fears. Especially early on in your career, you might be advised to block the negative people out of your life. That is one way of doing it, but if you can free yourself from the influence of their opinions, you will create space for your own success and you will inspire positivity in others.

3. The leaders in your business believe in you.

Even if you do not yet believe in yourself, you can borrow their belief in you. I remember my mentors – even way back at the beginning of my career – believing in me and encouraging me beyond what I thought I deserved. Just as I was starting to gain some traction and momentum, one very important mentor of mine would introduce me to people as a future millionaire. I wondered in those early days if he said that about everybody.

Now as a leader, I may say something equally complimentary to a distributor in my business. I can assure you that I am careful with that praise. All these years later I know and understand exactly what he saw in me. He had observed that I was focused on my business and was determined to learn everything I could to succeed. That is why he introduced me as a future millionaire.

He was right... I have earned over a million dollars in this incredible profession and I am grateful for the leaders that surrounded me and believed in me while I was gaining the courage to believe in myself.

It is important to understand what it means to borrow someone else's belief in you. Well-informed, highly skilled leaders know exactly what to look for in a new distributor. They are searching for people who show up, are willing to do the hard work, and have a burning desire to succeed.

When we show up at events ready to learn, it does not matter where we come from or whether we speak well. It does not matter if we have a fully developed skillset. The people who came before us will see in us the potential and they will work with us to bring our success to fruition.

4. Everyone starts at the bottom.

When you attend company events and watch training videos, you are exposed to mentors, executives, and other successful individuals. You may wonder to yourself, "Where did they come from? Who was lucky enough to recruit them?" These folks dress so beautifully and present themselves with confidence. They are poised, articulate, and smooth. As you strive to be more like them, always remember that they were once beginners too. Nobody starts their career as a fully developed professional. With time and experience, you can become a major leader in your company, but we all start off following a trail that has been blazed by others.

5. You are enough *and* you can be more.

You are reading this book to learn how to be great in direct sales, and you are also learning how to be the best version of yourself. Over the course of this journey, you are becoming a better leader because of the sum total of everything you have undertaken to help you learn and grow: the events you attend, the books you read, the podcasts and audio training you listen to and the successful people with whom you associate.

As you strive for self-acceptance, remember to keep working on all of these learning processes. No matter how much you grow as a person and how much you achieve in your business, your career will only be satisfying if you continue to strive for growth. This is true even for people at the absolute pinnacle of success. Do not miss the opportunity to learn from other people and embrace your power to share the wisdom you have gained along the way.

Empowered Action

In this exercise, you are going to learn more about other distributors in your company. Write down what you learn from their stories.

First, choose three of the most successful distributors in your company and find out the following information: When did they get started in your company? Why did they get started in your company? What have they accomplished so far in building their direct sales business with your company? What did they do before they joined your company?

Next, choose three distributors that have come from similar backgrounds as you and learn their stories. Background can mean that they may have a similar education or lack of education as you, have come from a similar past career, had a similar childhood as you, or were faced with similar setbacks when they started their direct sales business. I want you to learn for yourself how these individuals that come from a similar background as you have created massive success with their own direct sales business.

Finally, choose three distributors that have accomplished with their direct sales business what you want to accomplish with your business. Learn how long it actually took them to reach the goal. Find out why it was important for them to succeed with their direct sales business. It is also important to learn what they had to overcome to achieve their goal.

When you examine the success stories of the distributors around you what you will find is that everyone has challenges. Company leaders have been where you are. It is not easier for you or for them. You will have your own unique success story to tell as you continue to make and reach new goals. Most important is to realize that the journey you are on right now as a fellow empowered entrepreneur will provide the inspiration for others that will come after. Your determination to take action in the face of personal adversity will help others create a clear vision for their own success.

Empowered Conclusion

I could have concluded that it would be impossible for someone with my life experiences to succeed. My shame of being the son of a teenage mother and my embarrassment of being so broke that I could barely afford the investment to get started. My humiliation of having failed at or given up on business ventures in the past. My guilt of dreaming to live a life beyond what my family and friends considered appropriate. Any of these could have prevented me from pursuing something higher. My unease of being around successful people and my dread that I would fail again could have broken me at any point in time.

All of those cognitive distortions could have convinced me that this opportunity was not for me. That distorted thinking weighed me down as I built my business. You will have your own distorted thinking. Every distributor in your organization will as well. Our life experiences do impact the degree of difficulty in moving forward. Our identity, our history, and the systems we are a part of all influence our starting point and determine those challenges that we face in taking action. We all come from a different starting point, however, that does not determine how far we can go. I have never met anyone who has succeeded in direct sales that did not have real challenges to overcome on their journey to success. Your pattern of thinking can determine whether these challenges become roadblocks or opportunities for growth and resilience.

Empowered Thoughts

"My past does not determine my future."

"What has happened to me does not determine who I am or what I can become."

"I am enough, and I can strive to be a better version of myself. The two are not mutually exclusive."

Your Empowered Affirmation

In the space that follows, develop a personal, strength-based affirmation to combat your negative thinking about challenges in your business.

Distortion 7: It Is Too Complicated

"Simplicity is the ultimate sophistication."
— Leonardo da Vinci

An hour outside of Reykjavik, Iceland I stood
beneath the northern lights in the freezing cold.
Nigel Tisdall once wrote "The aurora borealis is
a fickle phenomenon. A week can pass without a
flicker....then bang! The Northern Lights come
on like a celestial lava lamp." This was clear to
me as I stood below the incredible light dancing
in the sky. We had been cautioned that we may
not see the lights. Our tour guide assured us he
would do his best but ultimately it was up to
mother nature to decide if we would witness the
lights ourselves.

Many times I had stood at the edge of an ocean
and considered how small I felt in the context of
our vast planet, at this moment I was moved by
how small I felt in the larger universe. One tiny
person on one tiny planet in a far grander world
than I could have ever imagined before. I learned
that some people have been actively visiting
Iceland for years hoping for the perfect cloud-

free night, moonless sky, and of course the cooperation of solar flares so they could see this spectacle for themselves. For most people, the opportunity to see the lights does not come at the same time that they are standing there to witness it with their own eyes, yet on my first attempt, after a short time searching, I was able to experience this phenomenon first hand.

In these moments I do my best to be present while also looking for the lesson. As we drove back to the city that night the lesson was clear to me. Along with my wife, I shared that experience with the top distributors in my company. This trip was provided by our company as an incentive that we worked to qualify for over an entire year. Being in the right place at the right time to see the northern lights was our good fortune. We were lucky that night to have the needed elements of nature perfect for all of us to see the lights.

In addition to being lucky that night, what we also had in common was that we grew our individual businesses to this high level by holding tight to the simplicity of direct sales and not giving in to the temptation to make things unnecessarily complicated. Luck may be a needed ingredient to see the northern lights but luck will not help you much to build a successful direct sales business. Instead, you will need the power of simplicity.

Building a successful direct sales business allowed me to become more skilled as a presenter, communicator, trainer, and mentor. That did not happen overnight; it took time. In order to achieve this, I started by leading my team to the people and information that could help them succeed. I taught them how to be system dependent instead of depending on me for all the answers. This was important when I started building my team because I did not have the answers, nor did I have the experience that my upline leaders had. Plugging my people into resources provided by our team leaders helped them grow faster.

This business has taught me how to master this balance between one-on-one training and encouraging independence. As a result, many people on my team achieved ambitious goals very quickly. Some became six-figure annual earners before I did; some even earned their first million dollars before I did. I was thrilled for them because my business continued to grow as these people worked fast. It is important that you do not act as the lid on your organization. As you support your team, remember that their success is not about you. This is crucial in the beginning as you allow people to grow at their pace which might be much faster than yours.

One thing all successful direct sellers agree on is that the best systems are simple. The reality, however, is that people love complicated systems and beginners can get caught up in this paradox. It is easy to hide behind complexity, but when you deploy a simple, highly effective system, your business can grow exponentially.

Consider this simple five-step recruiting system:

Step 1: Provide exposure. Invite your prospect to watch a video, attend a webinar, go to a live presentation, or listen to a conference call. You should not be the one to give the presentation or explain everything. It frees you from trying to explain every little detail and keeps the process simple and duplicatable by new distributors.

Step 2: Follow up. After your prospect has watched the presentation, attended the seminar, or listened to the conference call, find out what they liked the best. I love to ask somebody, "What do you like best about what you have learned so far?" This technique is essential to the process. It is better to let your prospect tell you what the most interesting aspect of the business is to them. If you assume instead of asking you will not have nearly the same quality interaction. This allows you to learn something about your prospect and what motivates them. It is much easier to help someone get started in direct sales if you understand what drives them. It is important to learn about their purpose.

Step 3: Bring in a third-party expert. This gives your prospect the opportunity to ask important questions and see the business from a new perspective. They are able to learn that other people are willing to support them alongside you. The system goes from an abstract concept to something concrete. They will begin to understand that there is a big organization of professional leaders standing by ready to provide support.

Step 4: Sign them up. It is important that you understand the sign-up process in your company. Is there a paper form? Do you sign up on a mobile app or a website? Do you have to call the home office? The third-party expert who helped you with step three should be available in this part of the process too. It is important to be confident and competent as you sign people up.

Step 5: Teach the system. Now you can teach your new distributor to repeat the process they just experienced. The system is simple and easy to replicate, and you can do it.

All you have to do is teach them what we just did with them:

- *Provide exposure.*

- *Follow up.*

- *Bring in a third-party expert.*

- *Sign them up.*

- *Teach the system.*

Why does this clear and easy process seem to go against our instincts? Perhaps we feel better about ourselves when we have mastered something very complicated, and we are less enthusiastic when we master something very simple. Complexity gives you another excuse to not take action and an easy explanation for why things did not work.

Your ability to reach your goals is rooted in simplicity. This is the beauty of what we do. It is so simple that anyone can do it regardless of their level of education and experience, even if their time is limited by their job and personal obligations. It is so simple that *all of us* can get results.

If you choose to complicate your recruiting, the whole process falls apart. If you shift the focus away from your prospect and onto yourself, you will not be able to provide the support necessary to coach them to success.

This is where you must put in the extra effort to create and maintain balance. Direct sales is never about the individual. It is about the system; it is about the company and its tools; it is about the opportunity to work with other mentors.

When I accepted that it was not all about me, I gained the freedom to let go of my past. I was able to believe in myself as a coach and facilitator. I could teach new people a simple process and the supportive activities around that process. I did not have to be the star on the stage or the perfect presenter. I did not have to be the person with the million-dollar story. I could just be me and that was more than enough.

A component of keeping your simple system running is to make sure that there are always new people moving through the system. If you were to spend the day with me you would see that I add new people to my list of prospects every single day. The key is to grow your prospect list every single day, not once in a while, or whenever you feel inspired.

New prospects can be found on social media sites or in daily activities like grocery shopping. I am an introvert but I meet people and talk to them because ultimately, my goal is to serve them. Serving my community with my products and opportunity overrides feelings of discomfort while networking for my business. Whatever I am doing, I am open to an opportunity to add people to my list. Every single day.

In addition to adding prospects every day, I review the status of people previously invited to learn more about my products or opportunity. Many prospects for the opportunity have already purchased my product. I know that the best team members are happy customers and I am cultivating ongoing relationships so they are comfortable to engage in the opportunity when the time is right.

Busy people are the best candidates for my business. If I am going to recruit the busiest, most professional people I have to show them how aligning with me in a simple and duplicatable business model will give them time for what they value the most. Recruiting is about relationship building and the more I invest in the people that I want to work with the richer our shared business journey can be.

Keeping things simple is applicable to more than your recruiting system. I use the power of simplicity to develop myself.

In his book *The Slight Edge,* Jeff Olson offers two choices. The first option is to perform simple daily rituals and activities that seem to make no difference at the moment but compounded over time make all the difference in the world. The second option is to make daily errors in judgment creating a compound effect over time. You can invest in the future version of yourself by reading and listening to materials and engaging in behaviors that may not change your life today but will influence your outlook week after week, month after month, and year after year.

A big part of my ongoing strategy for developing as a leader is becoming more and more valuable to my potential team members. If you spent some time with me, you would see that I invest both time and money in becoming the leader people are seeking. It is easier to attract good people to you than it is to pursue those people. For this reason, I am always working on my personal development.

Every day I read at least ten pages of a good book — one that will challenge me to think bigger and become a better leader. Again, it does not have to be complicated. We do not have to read an entire book every day. Committing to ten pages per day over the course of a year yields multiple books completed and knowledge earned. I also listen to audio training daily. I intentionally make a simple choice by choosing training over music or news. I may not be able to tell you what the hit songs are or relay the fine details of the latest political scandal, but that has not caused me to miss out on any important opportunities. In the time it takes me to drop off my daughter at school, I hear encouraging information that makes a real difference in my life and my business.

I also practice radical self-care every day by investing in my physical, mental, and spiritual health so I can continue to grow as a leader. I prioritize this because when I am in a top mental and physical state of being I am more valuable to the people around me. By choosing to move my body at home or at the gym I am investing in a stronger body. By reading good books I am expanding my knowledge. Participating in my faith community brings about the awareness that I am part of something much bigger than myself.

I check in with my mentors and partners. It only takes a few seconds to send a text and let them know how I am doing. It is important to partner up with someone who has similar aspirations and who will challenge and motivate you. This person will hold you accountable as you work to reach your goals. They should be committed to helping you stretch your vision beyond your comfort zone. Throughout my journey, I have been fortunate to work with mentors who have earned millions of dollars in direct sales. I continue to nurture these relationships through my triumphs and struggles. If you neglect your support system you will drift away from these people. Our personal connections are an essential part of what we do and can be the key to success. It only takes a few moments to stay connected.

I envision a clear picture of the future using positive daily affirmations. Speaking out loud in the present tense is a way to condition my mind to accept the opportunities that reveal themselves along the way.

One of the most powerful truths I have learned from my personal development journey is just how much control I have over my thoughts and actions. I used to believe that life was something that happened to me by chance. Once I understood the power I have over my thoughts, I was able to set a course for the life I desired.

As I worked to improve my communications with new and current prospects, time was not the key factor. It was my intentional focus on the activity that mattered. I learned to be deliberate and use my time more wisely, increasing efficiency and productivity.

It is not complicated. When done correctly, direct sales is simple. The challenge is to maintain your commitment to a simple system and operate with the integrity to focus on your business with the time that you have available.

There is no boss to fire you for neglecting your responsibilities. If I choose not to read good books, listen to audio training, and work on self-care, there is no clear repercussion at the moment. It feels like it does not matter because nobody will witness my neglect. Our ability to keep the process simple is what allows our business to grow through the success of our organization. When we add steps and complications we lose the simplicity. When we lose the simplicity we rob our team members of the success they would otherwise experience.

Empowered Action

In this exercise, you are going to make sure that you are organized around the simple steps to building a direct sales business. You might feel like you have the system down in your head but it is very important to write down the specifics of each step in your system.

Write down the method of exposure that you are going to use for step one with each prospect. For example, if you are going to send prospects a video overview write down the website address of the video. If you are going to ask them to listen to an audio overview by telephone write down the number they will need to dial to access the presentation.

Write down your method of recording the names of the people that you have invited to learn more so you can effectively follow up with them in step two of the system. For example, an excel spreadsheet, index cards, or in a binder. Describe it completely in written form.

Write down the names and contact information of three people you can count on to act as your expert to answer questions for your prospects in step three of the system as discussed in this chapter. It is important that you know who you are going to be contacting and how you are going to reach out to them. Do you have to text-message them first to see if they are available or can you just call them? Are there certain days and times that they are available? Confirm with your experts and leaders and make note of these important details.

Write down how you are going to sign the prospect up when they say yes in step four, as described in this chapter. Does your company use a paper form for this step? If so, locate these forms. Are you going to sign people up on a website? Write down the website address you will need for signing up a new prospect as a customer and a distributor. Are you going to sign them up with a mobile app on your phone? If this is the method make sure you have the app on your phone and that you are comfortable navigating the signup steps on the app.

Write down your method for teaching your new distributor how to duplicate the system in step five. If you are going to meet them in person and teach them the system, write down what you will need. If this involves bringing them specific documents or supplies make a list of these items and make sure you have everything you will need. Prepare a toolkit that you can take with you and use when instructing new distributors. If they are going to be attending a live training in a classroom or online, make sure you have the date, location, and other relevant details recorded where you can easily access them. If the new distributor is going to access the training from pre-recorded videos make sure you have the website address, login credentials, or anything else needed to view the videos. Consider creating a document where you can keep all relevant information and have it easily accessible for responding to new distributors.

Now that you have written out the specific details of your system for acquiring customers and distributors, you should feel a higher sense of confidence around inviting prospects to learn more and get started. By following the system you will be doing the right activities. You can increase your own chances at success by inviting more prospects to participate more often, instead of looking for ways to complicate the system. When you are organized, you make the process more efficient and thus effective. Intentional action will be empowering for your business.

Empowered Conclusion

As a leader, I work to protect my distributors from the natural urge to complicate the system. I am also responsible for teaching them why it is so important to keep it simple. When new distributors join your team, they want to add their own personality to the process. They often believe that being an entrepreneur means being a pioneer and making their business unique. Leaders must train their distributors to understand that customizing the system will not lead to growth. The simpler the system and more consistent the communication around the system the more likely success becomes for everyone involved.

By changing your thinking, you can avoid unnecessary challenges in your business. If you stick to the basics, you will find success. It is a daily discipline and not a complication that empowers your business. Committing to these daily disciplines is simple, but not always easy. Ensure that you consistently check in with your thoughts and make sure you are not overcomplicating the process.

Empowered Thoughts

"I am building a global team of high achievers because I stay true to the system."

"My business grows exponentially because every distributor understands the simple system."

Your Empowered Affirmation

In the space that follows, develop a personal, strength-based affirmation to combat the negative thinking that complicates your business.

Distortion 8: No One Wants to Join My Team

"A life is not important except in the impact it has on other lives." – Jackie Robinson

"Is the flag still up?" That was the question my grandmother asked my grandfather every evening. She would call him at work trying to figure out when he would be home. When I was a kid he was the postmaster in his hometown of Proctor, Vermont. My grandfather had a long career in the United States Postal Service before he got that coveted hometown assignment. He was one of my heroes.

In those days, the post office, the barbershop, and the local market served as the social hub of our small New England community. The three businesses shared the ground floor of a beautiful historic building in the center of town.

My grandfather's home was a five-minute drive from the post office and he loved his work. That is why my grandmother made the call every night. The entire town knew that even though the post office closed at five o'clock if the flag was still up, my grandfather was inside. This meant there was still time to get stamps or a last-minute money order just by tapping gently on the glass to get his attention.

He loved serving his community, and from a young age, I watched him go above and beyond to help others. In fact, the reason he stayed late so many evenings was that he needed to catch up on his work from the day. Reports and paperwork duties that should get done during business hours were delayed so he could spend time talking with his customers. He knew everyone – their life stories, their children's names, their joys, and hardships. As a small-town public servant, he always went the extra mile.

Over the years I have heard legendary stories of my grandfather delivering packages in his personal vehicle at Christmas. He often drafted my grandmother into service to ride with him over Killington mountain to the mail transfer station in White River so that a letter or package that missed the truck could still get out that evening. These stories are told with great joy anytime someone talks about my grandfather and his post office.

When he reluctantly retired from the job, he found other ways to work in his community. He served in his church and visited friends in the hospital. Near the end of his life, when he was living in a nursing home, he continued to check on people living in other parts of the facility. My grandfather never wanted anyone to feel alone or forgotten and he used his limited energy and mobility to continue checking in on others.

People stood in line for hours to pay their respects at my grandfather's wake. The children and grandchildren of his friends who passed before him came to make sure their families were represented. He did not pass suddenly at a young age. He lived a long, full life and yet grown men and women wept as they said their goodbyes. It was as if no one could imagine they would live in this world without him being there.

I had the honor of speaking at his funeral. Over the years, I have spoken for hundreds of hours on conference calls and at live events. I am confident speaking in public and comfortable in front of a room full of people. None of that mattered on the day of the memorial service. No matter how long a person is with us, it is a loss when they die. My grandfather was the head of the family until he drew his last breath.

My effort to offer the right words to honor him was no easy task. In the moments before I stood up in the front of the church, I had so much to say that I became overwhelmed and began to panic. I walked up and stood beside my cousin who was also offering words of remembrance. While she spoke, I was able to collect myself. I took control of my breathing, and when it was my turn the words flowed freely.

I talked about how my grandfather taught and lead others by example. I spoke about how he would prioritize his family above all else. Along with my grandmother, he raised us all in the small marble church we were standing inside that day. I described how much he loved his vocation and his customers. I reminded everyone that by the time President Kennedy gave his famous speech challenging Americans to serve their country, my grandfather had already answered the call in the military, the national guard, in public service, in his church, and in his community. I shared about how he believed that if a job is worth doing, it is worth doing well and how he looked after the fine details to make sure things were done right.

After his funeral, I reflected on how my grandfather's values guided my approach to business and life. In the early days of my career, I did not prioritize the needs of my customers ahead of my own, and because of that, I did not experience success in my business. When I decided to put my customers first, my business grew. Similarly, when I ignored my personal relationships, I found myself out of balance, and financial success eluded me. When I placed the needs of my family and friends ahead of my business, my relationships became stronger and business did not suffer.

The remodeling and modernization of my grandfather's post office was respectfully delayed until his retirement. When the time came, his post office was carefully dismantled and rebuilt in the basement of the local historical society. It remains there today as a fitting memorial to a great man.

Like any enterprise, a direct sales business has customers who have needs and we fill them. It is

a business run by real people with families and
friends who deserve their attention and time.

When people are struggling to recruit new
distributors onto their team I know I can help
them. I had been in the exact same situation. The
vision I had for my business when I started
building my team was selfish. I dreamed of
money coming in every day from the efforts of
other people. I learned about leveraged income
and understood that a successful team would
lead to big money.

I was frustrated that people did not want to join
my team. I thought I was following the system
and yet I was not getting any results. I was indeed
following the system, but my intention was to
recruit people to serve my interests. When I
changed my focus and started behaving the way
my grandfather taught me as a child, the team
began to grow faster than I could have ever
imagined. As it turned out people actually did
want to join my team.

The lessons I learned from my grandfather were
inside of me but were dormant. They awakened
with a simple shift in focus. The shift came when
Danielle traveled with me to our annual

convention for the first time. When I experienced the event through her eyes everything realigned for me. She saw a totally different business than the one I thought I was building. I sold to customers and recruited distributors because of how it benefited me. I made sales to earn commissions and recruited distributors to gain leveraged income from the sales they made.

Danielle had an alternative perspective. From her point of view, the product helps the customer and the commission that you earn is the reward for serving. You share information about the product with someone because you see the value and impact of the product; it is the right thing to do. You share because you would do so, even if you were not getting a commission. She explained that the commissions would be a result of the number of people I served in this way. She also recognized that recruiting people allows you to pay forward the opportunity for business ownership, mentorship, and financial freedom. The leveraged income would be a result of helping other people achieve success. This simple shift in thinking created a radical realignment in my business.

I began to approach recruiting as a strategy to help more customers than I could help on my own. I recruited people with the intention of helping them gain access to the training, mentors, events, and tools that were provided to me when I got started. I put myself in a position to serve my customers and my team. What happened next was amazing. Our business started to attract people who believed in the mission of the company. I was no longer trying to recruit people who wanted to make some money. Instead, I was attracting people who wanted to make a difference. They were not focused simply on commissions, but on delivering a quality product to their customers while improving their own lives with a successful business.

While attending my first convention, I dreamed that I would someday stand on the stage in front of thousands of people. What I did not plan for, expect, or imagine was that many people on my team would be standing on the stage too. The subtle lessons from my grandfather coupled with the encouragement of my wife changed the spirit of my business. This continues to duplicate as members of our team share their wisdom and tell their stories, providing encouragement and insight to even more people. They operate in service to others too and we are able to have a positive effect on more people than ever before.

As a team, we have helped tens of thousands of customers gain access to a better life through our products. We have guided thousands of entrepreneurs on the direct sales journey.

My team members are able to stay home with their young children or aging parents. They have cast aside unfulfilling careers and transformed their lives. Some of the people I work with earn six-figure or multiple-six-figure annual incomes. Some have become millionaires.

Once you shift from a self-centered recruiter to a service-minded leader, you create the environment needed to attract the best and the brightest. Adopting a service focus for your customers and your recruits can create a world-class team of good people that do the right things with the highest integrity.

The benefits of building integrity, simplicity, and service into your team culture can be long-lasting. I remember the day when I was having lunch with my family while looking at the Atlantic Ocean just a few feet away when my phone rang. I could not think of a better place to get this call. I had been coming to Provincetown, a small town at the tip of Cape Cod, Massachusetts for several years, and my wife has been visiting her entire life. It is one of our favorite places in the world, a place that in the future may become our permanent home. When the phone rang I could see it was a call from my corporate office and I wondered for a split second if this was the call we had been expecting for the last couple weeks. I answered and heard a familiar voice from the internal recognition team. She was calling to tell me that Danielle and I had earned over one million dollars in income from our business and that the announcement would go out company-wide later in the day.

It would have taken me forty-eight years to make a million dollars in my last full-time job. Over those forty-eight years, I would run the risk of getting sick, getting hurt, and missing out on family events because I could not get time off. If I was lucky, I would have been able to retire as an old man. Instead, in a hand full of years with the power of our profession, my entire life moved in a new direction.

Right now I am earning money for activities I did back in those first days when I was just getting started. The best part is that the skills I developed along the way allow me to keep building a bigger business into the future. It allows me to keep seeing a bigger vision for the future, which lets me set larger goals and to strive to meet those goals.

My journey has been an empowering one. I have gained a sense of freedom and agency in my life beyond my highest expectations. I have time freedom and financial freedom that allows me to blend my work, my family, and service to the causes closest to my heart. I believe my grandfather knew exactly what he was doing when he was demonstrating how to take care of a customer with service above and beyond. I believe he was being intentional when he volunteered his time and energy to causes that he felt were important. He understood that his time to contribute directly on earth would be brief but his ability to continue making a difference could live beyond his years if he taught others how to serve as well. These are lessons he passed on to many of us and I am committed to continuing teaching and demonstrating the power of service with integrity now and into the future.

Empowered Action

In this exercise, you are going to determine how to shift your own business to a focus on service first. Start by listing three ways your product would benefit your prospect if they became a customer. Think about how it would help a potential customer improve their life and write down at least three examples. Next, list three ways that joining your team as a distributor would be a benefit to your prospect. Think about what you have already learned in this book about the powerful transformation someone can realize with a successful direct sales business and list at least three examples. Finally, list three ways you can serve family, friends, and your community with your product and opportunity. Whether it is directly or indirectly, consider how the benefits of your product and the benefits of entrepreneurial success create a positive result for those around you and write down at least three examples.

As you complete this exercise, you should clearly see that you can focus on service and allow financial success to be a positive by-product of serving others. Direct sales is set up to reward you for serving your customers and distributors. There is no need to pursue commission, pressure people that are not interested or otherwise be unprofessional. You can approach your direct sales business as a servant and reap a multitude of rewards.

Empowered Conclusion

You empower your business when you shift your thinking from "selling" and "being successful" to "being of service." How can you change your thoughts related to your *purpose*? When you show up in service, you completely shift the potential of your action.

Empowered Thoughts

"I am the leader that people are looking for and I represent the opportunity that can help them."

"Every action I take is in service to others. My financial rewards are in proportion to the number of people I help."

Your Empowered Affirmation

In the space that follows, develop a personal, strength-based affirmation to combat your negative thinking related to your purpose in building your business and your team.

Distortion 9: My Team Is Not Doing Anything

"Motivation is what gets you started. Habit is
what keeps you going." – Jim Rohn

The air smelled sweet. Not far away I could hear
the ocean waves splashing onto the rocks and
sand. The sun was rising over the horizon and
producing a beautiful orange glow. I drank a
delicious cup of hot coffee. I felt the keys on my
computer. All five senses were activated on this
incredible morning in Tulum, Mexico. The day
before we had flown from Boston to Cancun and
then rode the one hundred eighteen kilometers
down the coast to a hidden resort. In the weeks
prior to our vacation, I had come up with the
idea that I was going to write my first book on
the trip.

I had been thinking about writing and I had been
planning to write but I just could not seem to
start. This was going to be my chance. As I took
in my first quiet morning in Tulum I stared at a
blank page and wondered why I thought I had
any business writing a book. I had years of

personal development training and I recognized immediately that I was letting my insecurities talk me out of writing. I closed my eyes, settled my thoughts, and began to breathe intentionally. I placed my fingers on the keys of my computer and opened my eyes.

Over the next two hours, I wrote out the events of the robbery that had happened so many years prior in Rhode Island. A story that I had not talked about with anyone since and certainly never thought I would write about. I continued by writing a rough framework of the book based on live keynote training I had been doing over the previous year. The book in your hands right now was born on that Winter morning in Tulum.

I began coaching entrepreneurs because I realized that having access to an opportunity and instructions on how to build a business was not enough for the vast majority of the people.

It came to me when I was thinking about my frustration around consistently going to the gym. I knew that I needed to go on a regular schedule, make healthy food choices, and get enough sleep. I could keep it up and feel good about it for a few days or a few weeks but then I would somehow slip. Maybe I would have to stay up late and then the next day I was too tired to workout. Perhaps I was traveling and ate too many convenience foods on the road and now my energy was low so I did not feel like showing up for a workout.

One day would become two. Two days would become a week. Before I knew it I was starting all over again. It happened incrementally and I just did not notice until it was too late. I would get motivated to be in better shape and that would get me back to it but I was losing momentum before I could turn that motivation into the habit of living a healthy and fit lifestyle.

As a business owner, your energy is one of your greatest assets. As a successful direct sales professional you can enjoy incredible passive income in the future and it would be sad for you to build a significant passive income and not be able to enjoy it with the people you love the most. Self- care has helped me increase my energy and be able to give more focus to my business and my relationships. The stronger and better I feel the more capable I am to bring value to everyone around me. I do not want to miss a day of this incredible life that has unfolded around me and I now prioritize my health and wellness so I can be here to enjoy everything life has to offer.

My challenges with converting motivation to habit in the gym are parallel to the issues most of us face in building a direct sales business. If you do not engage in the daily disciplines of building your business today it does not hurt you today. That is why accountability is so important. When I was younger I had no problems staying in the gym because I was being held accountable by coaches, teammates, and my workout partners. If I was not showing up for workouts or practices I was letting a lot of people down that I knew were counting on me to give it my best.

In my direct sales business, no immediate penalty existed. One of the biggest downsides of losing motivation was the lack of income. The fact that it was not my full-time job made it easier to let things slip. A day or two would become a week or two and before I knew it I was starting all over again in my business and only then would the negative be clear. I lost my motivation, got distracted, and off-track before I could develop the habits I needed to take me all the way in my business.

There is a voice inside of me that attempts to make me feel bad about my current circumstances. It tells me that I am not good enough. It reminds me that others are doing more than I am right now. That voice is only loud enough for me to hear when I am not engaging habitually in the activities that I know I should be doing. When my habits are strong that voice is weak. When my habits are weak that voice is strong.

These pages you are reading are another great example. I wanted to share my story and I knew that this book would help people succeed in direct sales. I knew that I needed to write it, it was not going to magically leap out of my brain and onto the page. Every author I spoke with gave the same advice about getting my book written, write every day.

I would get motivated to write and I would do it for a day, maybe even for two days before my motivation would fade. I lost the motivation before it could become a habit and days, weeks, months would go by without a word written down. Because I was not in the habit of writing, whenever I would feel the motivation to get back to it, that voice inside of me would tell me that I was not a writer and I would never be an author. That voice suggested to me that people who have written books about direct sales have made more money than I have. The voice said that real authors have something meaningful to say. The voice made me think that my book would offer nothing of value to the world. I would allow this voice to murder my motivation and consequently, I would retreat.

This cycle continued until the magic day when I married a moment of motivation to the missing ingredient, accountability. My wife told me that a close friend of ours had helped edit books in the past. Danielle suggested that I should discuss working together on this book. I sensed my motivation growing but I could also hear those voices of doubt begin to grow louder.

A suggestion from Danielle turned into a friendly meeting. We decided to work together to get this book out of my head and into the world. As we discussed the book project my motivation continued to grow. The voices of doubt tried to get louder but something special happened this time, my new collaborator established a structure. She laid out milestones. She asked me to agree on deadlines that I was comfortable with and we scheduled a pattern of follow up meetings. In other words, I now had another person to be accountable to, and attaching accountability to my motivation drove me to figure out how I was going to stay on track.

Writing became my new daily habit. Every morning I would get up before the rest of my family and write. I did not check email, I did not do laundry or empty the dishwasher. I sat down and wrote. Some days the words came easily and some days it was hard but every single day I wrote.

As my writing streak grew from a few days, a week, then weeks the book took shape and the voice of doubt inside of me grew quiet. I had successfully connected motivation with habit. I was waking up before my alarm went off with what I was going to write already in my conscious mind just waiting to be written down.

The habit created speed and ultimately ninety percent of the book was written in a fraction of the time that the first ten percent took. The toxic cycle of motivation being destroyed by self-doubt had been defeated.

In my direct sales business, I had to overcome the same challenges that I faced with my desire to remain physically healthy, and my desire to complete my first book. I needed to turn my motivation for a successful business into the daily habits that would make my dreams a reality. First, I had to identify people that I could be accountable to in my life. I began by listing those people. Next, I determined how I would be letting those people down if I did not maintain the daily activities that would lead to success. Finally, I crafted a plan to keep these people informed of my goals as well as my progress.

First on my list was my wife. She had helped me imagine the goal of earning a six-figure annual income. It was easy to see how I would be letting her down if I did not give my best; it would affect our family financially now and into the future. Finally, with her help, we agreed on a daily check-in together where we would discuss how business was going and whether or not we were on track to reach our goals. It was helpful as I worked on my business each day to know that I was going to be reporting and discussing my activities with her the next morning.

I built similar accountability relationships with my mentor as well as other distributors. With each of them, I repeated the same technique of identifying who they were, what it would mean to them if I let them down, and how I would communicate my goals and progress.

Once I had my personal accountability program in place my recruiting began to increase. As the number of people on my team grew I expected that the sales of the team would grow as well. I was surprised when it did not happen that way. I found myself frustrated again. I remember confiding in my mentor that my team was not doing anything and how disappointed I was that after finally breaking through and becoming a top recruiter it was not translating into increased production like I thought it would.

Over the years, I have worked with many people whose businesses arrived at this familiar stage.

They too felt the weight of finally getting the numbers of people on their team to grow but not seeing a growth in new customers from that increase of new distributors.

When I brought this issue to my mentor he helped me to understand what was missing. He helped me realize that direct sales is a people building business. We do not just recruit people, we build them to a new level of personal development. We build the people first, then the people build the business. This was a revelation but it did not make me feel any better about the situation until I studied the issue a little bit more. Instead of trying to relay all of the ways I was being coached, trained, and mentored by the team leaders I looked for the one thing that I could do with all of my new distributors that would give them the same access to information and personal growth that I was receiving.

Imagine a highway filled with dominoes. Each one carefully stood on end. Thousands of dominoes stretched out for miles. Each domino set with precision to make sure that when it falls it takes down the next domino as well. Assuming that you set the distance of the dominoes so that one falling knocks over the next and so on, you can predict with certainty what will happen to the final domino. You can cause the final domino to fall miles away from where you are standing by gently tipping over the first domino.

Every adult has probably watched a small or large line of dominoes fall in a pattern. Have you considered that the pattern would continue even if you could not see the whole line? The first domino falling causes the last domino to fall as well. You only had to gently topple one domino and yet it caused action and reaction for miles away beyond what you personally could see or hear. If you understand the domino principle you can comprehend how one person can build a global direct sales business with thousands of people producing millions of dollars in sales volume.

My weekly team accountability call is the first domino that I must tip over to create a chain reaction of positive results. Every week I dial-in to a conference call line and talk to my team. Thousands of people hear these calls by participating live or listening to a replay. My topics are informed by current incentive programs, bonuses, trips, time of the month, time of the year, and the next big event on our schedule.

My goal is always the same no matter what I present as a topic. I want people to see themselves as powerful over their current circumstances. I want them to create a clear mental image of a future version of their business that is bigger, more successful, and helps more people than in the current moment. I want them to borrow my belief in them and allow that belief to act as a tool to help them progress. The goal of each call is to inspire the individual, to motivate each and every one of them to expand their personal comfort zone and become habitual about the core activities in their business. However, I cannot do any of that if they are not listening to the call.

The distributors I work with personally understand that I expect them to be on the call. If they cannot be on live, they know that it is their responsibility to listen to the replay as soon as possible. That is the expectation and it is clear. It is the lowest level of participation in the business that I could come up with. It does not cost anything to listen to the call. It does not require you to leave your house. All that is required is that you listen.

That is the first domino. I must get my new team member to commit to being on the call from the beginning when they are most motivated. On those calls, they hear testimonials about the products and are encouraged to develop stories of the results they get from using the products themselves. They are invited to engage in the system and work personally with leaders. They hear about the power of our international convention and why it is so important that they join us at the event. They hear that regardless of their background, circumstances, or challenges, they can have the success they desire.

My coaching program focuses on connecting motivation to the necessary accountability as well as identifying the first domino in your business. Next, we determine the other metrics that are important to track, including a focus on self, health, wellness, and self-care. We identify the places that you can regain some of the time that is lost each day from lack of intentionality. We determine where you want to go in your business and how long you want it to take to get there. From there, we can agree on how accountability will be handled once motivation has faded, identify the habits that are most important, and get them down in writing where both parties can clearly see what was decided.

Having personal accountability and identifying my first domino has allowed my team to grow across the country, the continent, and eventually around the world. As it turned out recruiting did lead to increased production once I understood the power of building people by plugging them into the system and allowing them to grow into successful direct sales entrepreneurs.

Empowered Action

In this exercise, you are going to create your accountability plan for you and your team. First, identify the one domino in your business that can lead to all other important aspects falling into place. In your company, it could be a weekly online training provided by your company or your team leaders. Choose an event that is held weekly and accessible by people without the need to travel and attend an event in person. the minimum level of participation that the largest number of people can commit to on a regular basis. Write down the details of this weekly event and put it in your calendar as well.

Next, determine how you are going to communicate to your team the expectation that they attend this event. You can call or text message them a reminder before the event. You can also message them in the first few minutes of the event to confirm that they are attending. I also recommend that you message your team members after the training is finished to let them know how excited you are about what was just discussed. Write out your plan for how you are going to keep your team connected to this weekly event.

Finally, write down your accountability partners along with the important details we outlined in the chapter. List the three people you can be accountable to in your business. This can be family members, your sponsor, and your upline leaders. Write down each person and a detailed description of what they would gain by you having a successful business as well as how you would be letting them down if you neglected your business.

This is very important because you are far more likely to give focus to your business when you are clear about the people that are counting on you. Write out a clear plan for each person on your accountability list on how you are going to stay in contact with them. If it is your spouse or another family member that may be an in-person discussion a few times per week. If it is your sponsor or upline leader it could be a text message or an email with updates on your progress a few times per week or even daily. Create your accountability plan and focus your attention on staying in communication with the people you have listed.

Identifying a plan around the one domino in your direct sales business and crafting an accountability group for you personally will empower you to act with purpose in your daily life.

Empowered Conclusion

When we engage in overgeneralization and negative or catastrophic thinking about our team, we miss all of the positive action that is taking place. We also miss the potential to help team members and ignore our capacity to meet team members where they are in order to help them determine their trajectory forward. When we give power to the thought "my team is not doing anything", we in fact empower such thinking into reality. What if, instead, we focused on the resilience of our team members? In doing so, we empower the potential for transformative change.

Empowered Thoughts

"I am a model of intentional action and daily discipline."

"I fill my vessel first and model radical self-care to my team."

"I see the best in each of my team members and empower their success."

Your Empowered Affirmation

In the space that follows, develop a personal, strength-based affirmation to combat your negative thinking in relation to the resilience of your team.

Distortion 10: No One Will Help Me

"Individual commitment to a group effort--that
is what makes a team work, a company work, a
society work, a civilization work."
— Vince Lombardi

I had watched a corporate video that profiled his
success story and heard his voice a dozen times
on our team conference calls. He had made
millions of dollars in this business. The video
played in my mind as Bill Charron, my longtime
friend, and very first recruit, and I turned off the
main road onto the longest paved driveway I had
ever seen. There were pristine white fences
bordering tree-lined sprawling fields. The same
spectacular ranch property from the video
appeared before my eyes.

Minutes later we walked through the door of the
3000-square-foot office he built on the ranch
near his beautiful home. He designed a life where
his career and family existed together in the best
possible way. Everything was inviting and
impressive. I saw and experienced what the life
of a real millionaire looked and felt like.

When his assistant met us and walked us into his
office, he jumped up from his chair and greeted

us with a welcoming smile and an enthusiastic handshake. He was a giant of a man, much taller than I had expected.

Mark Riches started his business at twenty-eight years old just like I did. He was in a tough financial situation, but he was coachable and he listened to the mentors who made themselves available for advice. I was determined to do the same.

After a brief meeting, Bill and I said goodbye and headed to a nearby hotel. We were in town for a weekend of training led by Mr. Riches and the top people in his organization. We were excited about the training but we could not stop talking about how it felt to meet our team leader and that he wanted to help us succeed.

I learned so much during that first weekend in Cookeville, Tennessee. At a hotel conference center, trainers who had earned millions of dollars with their businesses shared everything we needed to know. They inspired us and challenged us to imagine a future of abundance that would replace our current circumstances of scarcity.

I met leaders who effectively used direct sales as a vehicle to change their lives. They did not have specialized skills or education. They were regular people and my eyes were opened to the idea that if they could do it, I could do it too.

Throughout my life, I had been taught that wealthy people had an advantage that allowed them to be wealthy. They inherited the money, they went to great schools, and they knew the right people. I was told over and over again that financial success required something that I did not have and could never access.

Among the people I knew, it made more sense to settle for a good job with good benefits. I was conditioned to believe that I should be grateful for what I had and it was shameful for me to want more. I learned the truth that weekend in Tennessee. The people I met were living proof that success is achievable without the advantages I had believed were necessary. I looked deeply at myself and reasoned that I too was coachable, had a burning desire to succeed, and was definitely willing to do the work.

I am grateful for my sponsor in this business. He did not need to do much to help me except open the door to this opportunity and then lead me to the people that could help me get to the top. He told me that if I was serious about my business I had to be there in Cookeville. I took that advice and that is exactly what I said to Bill. He was on my list – actually, he was at the top of my list. He took my call, took the meeting, and agreed that this was the right thing for us to do together.

Over the next several weeks I caught him up on all the details about the big training event. We looked at the map and estimated that it would take about fifteen hours to drive one thousand miles from Rutland, Vermont to Cookeville, Tennessee. We calculated our costs to the penny. We drove straight through only stopping for gas and taking turns sleeping. There would be no hotels or unnecessary expenses along the way. In the short term, it would have been easier and much more comfortable to stay home.

Spending money to drive so far away without a clear understanding of what we would learn was a risky notion. If Bill had not been willing to go with me I probably would not have gone either. Something was pulling us to get there and we made it happen.

Before I met the trainers at that event I was struggling to figure out how to build a team. I knew about the successful team leaders in my company and I was ready to do what they had done. I found out very quickly that recruiting and motivating a team can be challenging. I had made a list of people that I thought would be great. Some were people that I had referred to the product early on before I was even a distributor, and some were the customers that I signed up as soon as I got started. I was anxious to sit them down and show them the business opportunity.

I expected that most of these people would be excited about getting started. I thought that they would be as motivated as I was to earn an additional stream of income, but most were not. In fact, I struggled to sign up new people for my team and that was nothing compared to the struggle of convincing new distributors that did sign up to focus some time and attention on their business. I was concerned that I would not be able to get my team off the ground. Other than Bill, it seemed like no one was serious. I eventually decided that recruiting a team was a distraction that was preventing me from signing up more customers for my product. It was costing me time and energy that I could not afford to waste.

That weekend of training confirmed what I was doing right, showed me what I was doing wrong and the actions I could take to correct the errors I was making. I took pages of notes and things became so much more clear. Without that event, I probably would not have lasted long enough in my business to succeed. I may have added my direct sales business to the long list of things I tried before settling down to one of the few jobs available to me in my small town. Instead, I learned that I was surrounded by people that already knew exactly how to build this business and they wanted to share it with me to help me succeed.

Some people that are struggling to build a successful direct sales business believe that they cannot get any help. They will say that their sponsor will not help them or their upline is too busy. This is a delusion. They are holding a fixed, false belief, despite overwhelming evidence to the contrary.

The direct sales business model works so well because your sponsor and your entire upline support team have a vested financial interest in your success. It is the responsibility of each of us to ask for that help and to stay connected. Some of the most successful upline leaders have global teams of thousands of people, yet they can still help you. They have time to help you because most of those thousands never ask for help. Do not assume that no one is willing to help because the leaders are not reaching out to ask if you need help.

Direct sales is a business, it is not a job. Some people are building spare-time, some part-time, and some as a full-time career. Your upline leaders are eager to help you but it is up to you to take the initiative to show up at the training live or online, to reach out directly and ask for help and to stay in contact going forward once you get their attention.

In addition to your team leaders, you will also benefit greatly from seeking out the advice of professional trainers within the direct sales profession. It was purely by accident that I stumbled across a podcast on the topic of recruiting for the direct sales profession. The hosts of the podcast were interviewing a man named Todd Falcone. I was immediately connected to Todd as soon as I heard him speak. He had a wealth of information to be sure, but it was more than that. It was the delivery—the way he spoke and trained. It was what he said and also how he said it. It was all of it. I learned from that interview that Todd also had his own weekly training call and I could not wait to dial in and hear more training from this new resource.

From that point on I would dial into his call every week. I read everything on his website that was available for free and I thought very seriously about investing money on some of the training materials he had available for sale. I was a bit hesitant at first because I had never purchased training from an industry expert. My decision to buy that first training series became instrumental to the future of my direct sales career.

I anxiously awaited the arrival of that training by mail, and I began listening to the CDs in my car on the long commute to and from my job. I was hooked. The material and the delivery gave me more confidence than I ever had before. I felt a new level of optimism about my business. From Todd's training, I gained the ability to evaluate the current state of my business compared to where I wanted it to be, and the courage to take the necessary actions to get there.

After some time learning with Todd's materials and weekly conference call, I decided to reach out to him. My gratitude for his work compelled me to share my story with him. I wanted him to know that I was delivering furniture and appliances all day and listening to his audio courses as I drove between each stop on my route. As time went on I celebrated each milestone in my business and shared it with Todd. I wrote and told him how I decided to leave my job and transition to full-time direct sales. I remember telling him when my weekly income surpassed the monthly income from my former job. I shared story after story as my business continued to prosper.

Eventually, I was able to tell him the very best stories—the success stories of people in my team. No longer was it about what I was able to achieve; now it was about their success. People came into my organization and became top producers. It was astounding to think that at one point I was frozen, struggling to figure it all out, and now the team was growing.

I simply cannot tell my story without sharing how much Todd Falcone and his training helped me to believe in myself and focus on my future. I am here today because Todd Falcone decided to be a coach and mentor to the entire direct sales profession.

I continue to look for opportunities to invest in my business. I have a library of books and training in various forms of media from some of the top experts in the fields of sales, personal development, business, and leadership. I love to read and re-read these materials. These people inspire me and even though most of them have never met me, they have greatly influenced my life and career.

It can be easy to dismiss expert training as unnecessary. My company provided access to excellent tools and training, so why purchase anything else? Great training from experts outside of your company provides a fresh perspective on how to approach your business. It is a learning process for us as leaders to realize that there are many correct ways to build a direct sales business. If you want to find the method that makes sense for you, it is wise to invest in the expertise of people who have come before you. These experts can be an additional valuable resource along with your team. These great leaders also have a vested interest in your success. They want you to win just as much as your team leaders.

Remember, your team leaders want to help you. The direct sales compensation model rewards their effort with income. That means it is not a distraction from their core business to help you, it is their core business. It is faulty logic to think that your team leaders are too busy or are not willing to help you.

If you are feeling unsupported consider your behavior so far. If you have not been participating in training online or in person, you are not asking for help, you are asking for your team leader to teach you, one-on-one, the skills you could have been learning along with the rest of the team. Too often, people ignore the conference calls, webinars, and live classroom training while at the same time expecting the team leader to personally relay the same information to them privately. Some team leaders have hundreds or thousands of people in their organization. If they had to teach every person individually every concept they would not have enough time. The reason that so many team leaders and trainers are able to work with a global organization is that they can relay the key information to the entire group at once through training platforms first and then work individually with distributors that need help with clarification or support around a specific topic.

Empowered Action

Start this exercise by writing down the names of your sponsor and the upline leaders in your organization that want to help you succeed with your direct sales business. Next to each name write down where they live, their contact information, and how long they have been with the company. Keep this list where you can easily access it at any time. These are the people that are most capable to help you when you need support. It is possible that your sponsor may be almost as new to the business as you are. If this is the case, you will also want to stay in contact with the most successful leaders in your upline support team. Determine if your team has a regularly scheduled live training event. It could be once per year or more often. Write down the dates of the next event and the location. Get the details on how to register for the event and if it is open to all distributors or if there is a qualification requirement to attend. Finally, register for the event and if necessary, make your travel arrangement to attend. This is a great opportunity to meet the leaders of your team outside of the larger international convention events that your company holds. Remember, it is your responsibility to build connections with your team leaders. Reach out so they know what your goals and aspirations are and to keep in contact as you continue forward in your business.

Empowered Conclusion

There will always be leaders ready to help you, but you need to be open to help. Explore your distortions related to support. Where is support available that you are not taking advantage of? Where are you not taking action? No one will build your business for you, but the universe, and your leaders, do reward those who take action. Notice where you can invite in more intentional action, and notice the power of the response that you get.

Empowered Thoughts

"I am a student that is ready to learn and leaders are ready to help me."

"I deserve to be mentored because I apply what I am taught."

Your Empowered Affirmation

In the space that follows, develop a personal, strength-based affirmation to combat your negative thinking about the support that you receive.

Jim Tanner

Distortion 11: I Do Not Need Any of That Rah-Rah Stuff

"It is important to surround yourself with people who lift you up, encourage you, share your vision and inspire you." – Les Brown

One thousand five hundred miles. It took over twenty-four hours to drive non-stop from Vermont to Oklahoma City. I had been busy recruiting and was able to convince a friend from work, a member of my small team, to make the drive with me. We took turns sleeping and drove in shifts. Upon arrival, we were equally exhausted and excited. We met up with Bill Charron and the three of us shared the experience of our first international convention.

Money was tight. We shared a hotel room miles from the arena, ate cheap fast food, and watched every dollar. Honestly, by the time I arrived in Oklahoma City, I did not have enough money to get back home. I was counting on a direct deposit from my delivery job to cover my share of the expenses for the return trip.

I learned a lot that weekend, and the first lesson was that there are people who will do whatever it takes to get to the big events. As far away as our hotel was from the convention site, we were not the only distributors staying there. Rooms were fully occupied with people from all over North America who had traveled to the convention. Of course, there were people staying in fancy upscale accommodations near the arena, but there were also people sleeping in their cars. Some rooms were filled with people sleeping on the floor and in the bathtub. They did whatever it took to get to the convention to learn from their leaders.

Over the years I have been told every reason in the world why someone cannot attend the international convention, but for every excuse laid out by one person, another has overcome an obstacle and made it there anyway.

Attending these important events not only helps you develop a belief in your business, but it also allows you to demonstrate your belief to your team and leaders. I have total respect for the people who get to their convention because I know that it is often a challenge and a sacrifice to make it happen.

The thousands of attendees in this sold-out arena were seated in order of their accomplishments in the company to date. Our seats were as far away from the stage as you could get. Some people do not like this seating system, but I truly appreciated the visual representation of my ongoing journey. I was on a mission to move from the nosebleeds to the center of the arena near the stage where all the millionaires sit. Over the years I have done exactly that, progressing from the balcony down to the mezzanine, to the floor seats and finally to the front rows.

It is now my practice to take some time with my up-and-coming team members before each event begins. I like to bring them down from their seats onto the floor and walk them up to the front. I want to help them envision this forward momentum in their business.

Big decisions are made at these events. As a leader, if I can help my team get to these events, they will make the big decisions that propel their lives forward. It can be a battle to get people to invest the time and money to get there. It is often a challenge to convince them to step outside their comfort zone. Still, I make this effort for months leading into every event because I know how important it is to their future in the business.

Why is it so important? Is it the loud and exciting music, the balloon-drops, or the celebratory atmosphere? Is it the "rah-rah stuff" as some people say? Not at all. I love to have fun but the fun is only one aspect of the event.

At conventions, I have heard from keynote speakers who are current and former attorneys general, governors, and members of congress who affirm that what we do is important. This type of assurance from respected government officials is critical. A company that is functioning in the shadows or operating unethically certainly does not have the state attorney general on stage proclaiming the noble efforts of the field sales force.

Some of the most influential authors, trainers, and speakers have been the keynotes at these big events. In recent years, I have been trained by Grant Cardone, John C Maxwell, Mel Robbins, Jack Canfield, and Robin Arzon, just to name a few. These are inspirational mentors that I may never have otherwise had the opportunity to learn from. I am able to benefit from their knowledge at these events. People pay thousands of dollars to attend workshops held by these mentors but my company brings them to me for the small cost of a convention ticket.

Each year my Chief Financial Officer reports the successes of the company as well as the financial position from the most recent year and quarters. Do not underestimate the importance of aligning with a reputable company that is on strong financial footing and has stood the test of time. If you are unable to easily find this type of financial reporting, you will have difficulty developing a sense of belief in your company and leadership.

I was fortunate to find a company that has existed for decades, is worth over a billion dollars, and is backed by financial partners with billions more. This means that the promise of building a business with real passive income is possible for me and my fellow distributors. It means that the business I am creating today can benefit generations of my family in the future.

A major benefit of attending the annual international convention is the celebration of individuals who are achieving high levels of success in our business. It is important to know these stories and apply them to your own development. Hearing from real people as they share their journey inspires and motivates the rest of us in attendance that we can do it too.

At my first convention, one of the awards presented was in recognition of a man who had earned one hundred thousand dollars in a single month. That was a mind-expanding moment for me. I realized that if he could build a business that allows him to earn that much income in a single month, I was part of a business model that certainly offered me the opportunity to change my financial future. I arrived in Oklahoma City without enough money to get home but I left with a clear understanding of the true potential of my opportunity.

Most direct sales companies host an annual convention with anywhere from a few hundred to tens of thousands of people in attendance. This is your opportunity to see all of the top leaders together in one place. Imagine the power of sitting in a stadium filled with people who are all actively involved in the same business opportunity as you. It is not just in the arena that you will meet and speak with other distributors, you will also be able to interact with them in the hotel, at every meal, at the airport, and even in the elevator. Be prepared for these unprogrammed moments. They provide the chance to learn one-on-one from the best in your business. Have your questions ready.

Now, fast forward to the close of each big event. What happens now? It is actually very important how you approach this. As you board the plane, hop on the bus, or get in your car to head back home after your first convention, I highly recommend taking time to reflect on all you have learned. Take out your notes from the event and review them. Identify a few key lessons to focus on. Make a plan to take action on those lessons right away.

What you've learned at the convention will exponentially help you grow in your business and will enhance your ability to sell more products and recruit more new distributors. Your belief in all aspects of your business is getting stronger, however, your family, friends, and prospects have not been experiencing what you have. In other words, you have changed but they are the same. They have not attended the event with

Jim Tanner

you. They have not had this life-altering experience. I strongly urge you to bring your spouse or partner with you to these events but if that is not possible please realize that they will not immediately understand the energy and sense of purpose you are returning with.

Anyone who was negative about your business before the convention is probably still negative when you get home. You cannot expect the people in your life to keep up with the improvements you are making if they are not living through those experiences with you. If your team did not attend the event you cannot expect them to be more motivated just because you are more motivated. Use your excitement, belief, and motivation to prospect more people. Guide them with patience and understanding that they have not yet experienced what you have.

As a team leader, it is my goal to get people to attend these events. Over the years I have been told many times by new distributors that they do not want to go to the event. They say they do not need any of that "rah-rah stuff". While this is an overgeneralization of what happens at live events, it is true that attending training can be motivational. We all need to be re-energized from time to time, to be reminded of our passion and our purpose. Events also provide an opportunity for connection, the value of which cannot be underestimated. It takes effort to get somewhere new. Transformation comes when we challenge ourselves in new ways. Ask yourself how your limited thinking is getting in the way of radical transformation.

Empowered Action

Write down the dates and location of your company's international convention. Like you did for your team event, commit to attending the event by registering right away. Depending on the location you may be traveling to the event by airplane, bus, train, or car. Make your travel plan and purchase tickets as needed. Make your hotel reservations as well.

Once you are fully committed by having your event ticket and your travel plans in place, contact your sponsor and your upline leaders and inform them that you are going to be attending. Do not contact them before you make the above arrangements. By registering first and then informing them, you are showing them that you take action in your business.

Finally, inform the distributors in your team that you are registered and that you are going to the event. Direct every member of your team to register as well. They are more likely to register and attend once they learn that you have made the commitment.

Getting your team of distributors to the major events will grow your business dramatically. It all starts with you. If you are not registered, you will not promote the event to your team with energy and excitement. By registering immediately for the event, you are creating a comfortable environment for promoting the event to your team as well as an expectation that they should be joining you at the event.

Empowered Conclusion

Motivation and connection create an environment for transformation. Major company events are carefully planned and executed to provide valuable training along with an atmosphere that can shift the individual's vision of their direct sales business in meaningful ways.

Empowered Thoughts

"I will attend transformative events because I am worthy of transformation."

"I learn from the leaders so that I can lead."
"I seek connection with others because I know doing so empowers my success."

Your Empowered Affirmation

In the space that follows, develop a personal, strength-based affirmation to combat your negative thinking about attending transformative events and training.

Jim Tanner

Conclusion: If It Worked, Everyone Would Already Be Doing It

"Teachers open the doors, but you must enter by yourself." – Chinese Proverb

Direct sales does work. I believe that everyone should be building their own home-based direct sales business and providing a new source of income to their household. The vast majority of people, however, are not building a direct sales business. It turns out that direct sales does work but everyone does not participate. As you learned in this book, people hold tight to cognitive distortions that prevent them from understanding the scope of a direct sales opportunity.

People believe that they do not need to consider a direct sales opportunity if they already have a job. They believe, mistakenly, that having a primary source of income disqualifies them from having additional sources of income. Starting and growing a direct sales business and bringing more income into their household reveals options, choices, and experiences that most have never considered. A direct sales business can be an alternative career path or it can be an enhancement to a career path. That is one of the many choices available to the individual that takes action and builds their own direct sales business.

People believe that a direct sales business requires the skills of a professional salesperson. They mistakenly believe that they would need to love sales and the processes of traditional selling. They imagine that they would suddenly have to become pushy and pressure people to buy something that they do not want to purchase.

Traditional sales skill has little to do with your ability to succeed in direct sales. The profession of direct sales does not focus on high-pressure sales tactics. Direct sales is based on the sharing of product experiences. As a distributor for a product, the most important thing is that you use the product and have positive outcomes. So positive in fact, that you would gladly recommend the product to your friends, family, and neighbors without the motivation of earning a commission for doing so. When you recognize the unique value and purpose of your product or service, you recognize that sharing is an act of service, not sales.

People think that you have to get in early to succeed in direct sales. They see a company that has been around for decades and, instead of recognizing the strength of aligning with a company with a proven track record, they believe that they missed out on the opportunity to position themselves properly for success. These people may instead align with every new and exciting pre-launch opportunity that promises a financial windfall that can only be realized by getting in on the ground floor. They may repeat this process over and over as new companies rise and fall in direct sales. Whether the company is a startup or has been around for a generation, what matters is the attention a distributor brings to their business. Success is not determined by how long the company has been around or how long a distributor has been in a company.

People believe that they are too busy to engage in a part-time business. They have convinced themselves that a direct sales business would take time away from the people and activities that are most important to them. Building a direct sales business the right way can be done part-time or even in your spare time. Most importantly, a successful direct sales business can open doors to gaining more time for the people and activities that matter most.

People believe that their past determines their future. They do not understand the power over their future that they command. If they knew how much they could shape their destiny by starting or restarting their direct sales business, they would act immediately. Instead, they tell themselves that because they did not have the results they hoped for in the past they should not start again. Instead of seeing their past experiences as a learning opportunity, they see them as confirmation that a direct sales business does not work.

People believe that the top producers in the company had a special advantage that was not provided to the rest of the distributors. They believe those top earners had advantages provided to them by their family, their education, or their social networks. The person believes that the success of others does not prove they too can have success in the profession of direct sales. Every top producer in every direct sales company has a different story of how they climbed from the bottom to the top. The common theme that ties all of the top producer stories together is that they had challenges to overcome and they made the decision to keep going. They did not let the setbacks that they experienced before they started their business or while they were building their business prevent them from reaching their goals.

People think a direct sales business will be complicated. They are looking at the business from the outside without the knowledge of what the simple components of a successful business really are. In reality, the reason so many ordinary people are able to have extraordinary results around the world is that the best direct sales businesses are defined by their simplicity. By mastering a few simple skills and repeating the daily activities consistently, virtually anyone can build a global direct sales business.

People think if their team is not growing it is because the opportunity is not as exciting as they had thought. These people begin to feel frustrated and jump to the conclusion that building a sales team does not work. They tell themselves that other people are not interested in the opportunity. Often, the person is simply repelling instead of attracting potential new distributors. This occurs when motivation is personal financial gain. Making a simple shift to focusing on serving the world with a product and opportunity will make for a far more attractive leader, which in turn will make the opportunity more attractive to others.

Some people think that if their distributors are not producing new business up to the expectation it is because they are lazy and unmotivated. These people determine that building a team of distributors does not work because the distributors will not make more sales or recruit more distributors. These people do not understand the increase in motivation, production, education, and excitement that comes from making sure their distributors are participating in the team training event each week. Their team's motivation and action is also a direct reflection of their own motivation and action. By making weekly virtual meetings an important expectation to all of the distributors, information and inspiration become easily accessible to all. A distributor can live across the street or across the globe from the team leaders and they all get the same information at the exact same time.

People believe that if they are in business for themselves they will be in business by themselves. They do not understand the vast number of experienced leaders that have a vested interest in helping them launch and grow their business. They cannot appreciate the wealth of knowledge that they can gain from the powerful, positive relationships that are waiting for them inside of the profession of direct sales.

People believe that direct sales is more hype than substance. They will point to the excitement of a live direct sales training event as evidence. What they do not see among the excited people and motivational messages is the powerful training that is being delivered to all in attendance. The person does not see the transformative nature of being in community with other like-minded entrepreneurs. They do not understand how these events allow the individuals in attendance to have moments of clarity that lead to a deeper understanding of their products and a more meaningful understanding of the potential of their business.

Throughout this book, you have learned about the ways people allow their own cognitive distortions to keep them from the change they are seeking. You likely learned ways you are holding yourself back, ways distributors in your team hold themselves back and you have learned steps you can use to overcome these false beliefs. Now it is time to take action. This is the moment that you make a decision to put yourself on a path to a future radically different from your past and your present. Massive changes have come from seemingly simple first steps.

On December 17, 1903, Orville and Wilbur Wright altered the course of history when they made the first controlled, sustained flight of a powered, heavier-than-air aircraft with the *Wright Flyer*.

On July 20, 1969, Neil Armstrong became the first person on the moon.

For two hundred thousand years humans walked the Earth and dreamed of flying through the sky. Once we achieved flight it only took sixty-six more years to step foot on the moon.

On May 6, 1954, Roger Bannister accomplished a feat that was thought to be impossible at the time. He became the first human to run a mile in under four minutes. The exact time was 3m 59.4 sec for Roger to do what everyone had agreed was not possible. His record stood for less than a year. Roger Bannister had shown the world it was possible to run a mile in less than four minutes, and once it was accomplished the real truth revealed itself and other runners came quickly to break the record. The four-minute barrier has since been broken by over 1,400 male athletes and is now the standard of all male professional middle distance runners in cultures that use Imperial units. In the 65 years since the mile record has been lowered by almost 17 seconds, and currently stands at 3:43.13.

So how long does it take to build a massive, successful direct sales business? That is up to you. The barriers have already been broken, the only limit is your own vision. You do not have to wonder if it is possible in your business to fly. Whether that be a few feet off the ground or all the way to the stars. You do not have to limit yourself to believe the four-minute mile is impossible in your business because it is being run before your eyes each and every day. All you have to do is decide to take flight. All you have to do is decide to run, to follow in the footsteps of those that have shown us what is possible.

I hope that I have helped you to change your thinking about direct sales. Perhaps you have been able to recognize and combat misperceptions you had about the profession. Maybe you were able to recognize distorted thinking that has held you back in your business. Most importantly, I hope that you recognize that you are in control of your thoughts. I invite you to intentionally and consistently pursue a mindset of abundance. Through mindful thoughts and intentional action, you have the capacity to empower your direct sales business.

Recommended Reading

Beach Money – Jordan Adler

No Cash No Fear - Terry Allen

Think and Grow Rich - Napoleon Hill

The Slight Edge - Jeff Olson

Fearless Networking - Todd Falcone

Live Your Dreams - Les Brown

Building an Empire - Brian Carruthers

Go Pro – Eric Worre

The Four Year Career - Richard Bliss Brooke

Dare to Get Rich - Larry Smith

30 Ways in 30 Days - Steve Melia

The Five Major Pieces to the Life Puzzle - Jim Rohn

21 Irrefutable laws of leadership - John C Maxwell

Born to Win - Zig Ziglar

Crush It – Gary Vaynerchuk

The 10X Rule – Grant Cardone

Jim Tanner

About the Author

Jim Tanner is an author, business coach, entrepreneur, speaker, and million-dollar earner in the profession of direct sales. Jim makes his home with his wife and daughter in the suburbs of Boston, Massachusetts USA.

The "Jim Tanner Brand" of coaching and training is a unique tough love style approach with an emphasis on personal responsibility. Contact our office for virtual and in-person speaking and coaching. To book Jim, visit jimtannerbrand.com

Follow Jim Tanner on social media:
linkedin/jimtannerbrand
instagram/jimtannerbrand
facebook/jimtannerbrand
twitter/jimtannerbrand

Made in United States
Orlando, FL
01 April 2022

16382016R00114